# BEHAVIORAL OBJECTIVES
## The Position of
## the Pendulum

# "Behavioral Objectives"

## the position of
## the pendulum "

● ● ● ● ● ● ● ● ● ● ● ● ● ● ● ● ● ● ● ● ● ● ● ● ● ● ● ● ● ● ●

## Miriam B. Kapfer,
## Editor

EDUCATIONAL TECHNOLOGY PUBLICATIONS
ENGLEWOOD CLIFFS, NEW JERSEY 07632

**Library of Congress Cataloging in Publication Data**

Main entry under title:

Behavioral objectives.

    Includes bibliographies.
    1. Learning, Psychology of. 2. Behaviorism
(Psychology) 3. Curriculum planning. I. Kapfer,
Miriam B.
LB1051.B314    370.15'2    77-25988
ISBN 0-87778-125-7

Printed in the United States of America.

Library of Congress Catalog Card Number:
77-25988.

International Standard Book Number:
0-87778-125-7.

First Printing: February, 1978.

# The Authors

**Miriam Bierbaum Kapfer** is Research Professor, Department of Special Education, and Co-Director, Life-Involvement Model, Bureau of Educational Research, University of Utah, Salt Lake City.

**Paul L. Dressel** is Professor of University Research at Michigan State University, East Lansing.

**Philip G. Kapfer** is Research Professor, Department of Education, and Head, Eccles Health Sciences Learning Resource Center, University of Utah, Salt Lake City.

**Philip W. Tiemann** is Head, Course Development Division, Office of Instructional Resources Development, University of Illinois at Chicago Circle, Chicago.

**George L. Geis** is Associate Professor of Education and Director, Centre for Learning and Development, McGill University, Montreal, Canada.

**H.H. McAshan** is Professor of Education at the University of North Florida, Jacksonville.

**Sidney J. Drumheller** is Professor of Education at Drake University, Des Moines, Iowa.

**W. Robert Houston** is Professor, Department of Curriculum and Instruction, and Associate Dean, College of Education, University of Houston, Texas. **Allen R. Warner** is Assistant Professor, Department of Curriculum and Instruction, and Director of Field Experiences, College of Education, University of Houston.

**Fred C. Niedermeyer** directs Product Implementation studies at SWRL Educational Research and Development, Los Alamitos, California. **Howard J. Sullivan** is Associate Dean, Graduate College, Arizona State University, Tempe, Arizona.

**Terrence Piper** is Associate Professor of Special Education, Temple University, Philadelphia, Pennsylvania.

**Anita J. Harrow** is Director of Academic Affairs, Seminole Community College, Sanford, Florida.

**Reed G. Williams** is Associate Professor, Office of Curriculum Affairs and Educational Resources, Southern Illinois University School of Medicine, Springfield, Illinois.

# Preface

Pendulums have a way of swinging—both in physics and in education. As long as there is activity in a given area, there will be fluctuations of professional opinion regarding its nature, quality, use and potential.

The years of the Sixties and early Seventies saw a strong and persistent swing of the educational pendulum toward the use of behavioral objectives. Some educators have termed this upsurge of interest in formulating observable and measurable educational goals the "behavioral objectives movement." Others are more inclined to view behavioral objectives not as a "movement" as such but as one tool for use within the broader contexts of instructional design, educational management, administrative accountability, and the like. Whether or not one considers the behavioral emphasis in education to be a full-blown trend, this emphasis is at least a tendency of sufficient strength to warrant looking at it in longitudinal and futuristic ways from time to time.

Now appears to be an appropriate time to take such a look. In the first place, most educators at all levels are reasonably conversant about behavioral approaches and many educators are at least somewhat skilled in their use. That is, a look at behavioral objectives at this point in time need not start with basic writing techniques; a substantial amount of sophistication concerning behavioral methods may be assumed in the education profession at large.

Second, a cursory look at the current educational literature indicates that a turning point may be at hand with regard to behavioral objectives. There appear to be fewer how-to-do-it articles, fewer articles describing behavioral objectives in such-and-such school programs, and fewer unalterably polarized positions regarding the positives and negatives of the behavioral approach. Perhaps everything that is useful concerning the fundamentals has already been said.

Instead, there now appears to be more concern for exploring ways of redirecting the behavioral objectives impetus of recent years. In other words, some educators now seem to be saying that it would be unfortunate for the pendulum to swing away from behavioral objectives before their continued use in curricular and instructional development has had an opportunity to be guided in a number of potentially profitable directions.

**Forces Powering the Pendulum**

Over the next several years a number of forces may influence the direction and amplitude of the behavioral objectives pendulum. The skill with which educators deal with these forces will determine the future shape and effectiveness of behavioral technology.

For example, how can behavioral objectives better express outcomes regarding learning processes? Most educators would agree that both processes and content are important as educational outcomes. Most also would agree that process learning has not been as carefully or universally defined as has the more familiar content learning. As a result, the application of behavioral methodology to the area of process learning is not as advanced as it might be. Future work in this area may well include the development of mechanisms for encouraging student competency in the specific process behaviors that match possible learning purposes.

Another force that powers the pendulum has its origins in the performance differences between education and training. Education is often thought of as preparation for rewarding living in the all-encompassing sense, while training usually is perceived in terms of more definable objectives. Thus attempts at writing behavioral objectives that capture the more profound outcomes have been less frequent and perhaps less satisfying than have attempts at writing training objectives. Continued discourse on the structure and relationship of "holistic" and "atomistic" objectives may bring further progress in this area.

A third force involves the relationship between behavioral objectives and human motivation. Many published lists of behavioral objectives appear to have little motivationally-based organization. As a result, the student may have difficulty identifying at a personal level with such objectives. An ideal solution may be to retain the values of subject-centered curricula while at the same time taking advantage of the powerful motivational features of student-centered approaches.

The accountability movement represents a fourth force affecting the behavioral objectives pendulum. The issue revolves around the "what" of accountability. For *what* learning outcomes should students, teachers, and administrators be held accountable? The technology of behavioral objectives, with whatever limitations it may or may not have, immediately becomes involved in the dialogue. The political ramifications of accountability may require expanding the capacity of behavioral objectives to deal with all types of learning outcomes.

### Overview

The purpose of this book is to characterize the behavioral objectives movement and to assess its impact on the current educational scene. In addition, the authors in the book were asked to point to some new directions through a past-present-future analysis of behavioral trends. Major concepts were purposely not assigned in a uniform fashion to all authors. Rather, the exact focus taken by each author was determined, first, by the major ideas represented in his or her past writings and, second, by the modifying effects of time and experience on these personal frames of reference. The major thrust of each chapter is capsulized in the following paragraphs.

**Dressel** discusses the various origins of educational goals, including the "academic discipline," "personal development," and "student-generated" orientations. In an attempt to resolve some of the terminology, specificity, and observability problems related to goal setting in educational programs, Dressel outlines six critical long-term competencies for students. These are elaborated sufficiently to be useful as guides for curricular and instructional planning. Dressel concludes by describing a four-stage value-oriented program. His comments, although directed at the college level, also have implications for systematic programs in values development at the elementary and secondary levels.

**Kapfer** observes that physical and biological scientists have long dealt with both the visible and the invisible. Based on this perspective, he suggests that educators take another look at the feasibility of dealing systematically with both observable and non-observable behaviors. Kapfer then provides a definition of behavior that lends itself to dealing with covert as well as overt components of behavior. He demonstrates briefly the use of this definition in curriculum development, instructional planning, and evaluation design. The behavioral objectives that result from this approach incorporate acquisition of content, exposure and practice of appropriate learning processes, and development and use of positive motivational factors.

**Tiemann** makes a strong case for the derivation of instructional objectives by means of task analyses involving behavior chains and algorithms. He points out that such analyses are useful for complex cognitive learning as well as for lower level cognitive tasks. Tiemann defines complex cognitive learning to include (1) concept learning, (2) principle applying, and (3) strategy learning. Within this context, Tiemann responds positively to a number of concerns that occasionally surface regarding behavioral objectives. His discussion is aided by the use of clear and interesting examples from several curricular fields.

**Geis** notes that the "technology" of education was developed largely in settings that can be characterized as being primarily for training rather than for education, as these words are commonly understood. Thus, attempts to apply such technology in strictly educational situations have not always met with the ease and "fit" that might have been desired. Geis highlights major differences between training and education in terms of the kinds of instructional objectives and evaluation materials that might be appropriate in given situations. He urges teachers and full-time instructional designers (1) to use behavioral objectives where they do fit, (2) to use other systematic approaches to instructional design where behavioral objectives do not readily fit (e.g., in dealing with what Geis calls the broader "goals" of education), and (3) in either case, to give substantial attention to devising useful and productive methods of evaluation.

**McAshan** presents an essentially positive summary of the behavioral objectives movement. He deals in a constructive fashion with a number of current concerns related to writing and using behavioral objectives, and discusses the potential of the behavioral approach for revolutionizing teacher education in the future. McAshan is careful to distinguish between "learning" outcomes (the largely covert capabilities acquired through the learning process) and "behavioral" outcomes (the overt, measurable responses that the learner makes based on his newly acquired capabilities). In other words, McAshan uses "learning" outcomes to mean the ends of instruction, while "behavioral" outcomes are the indicators or ways of measuring whether or not the ends have been achieved.

**Drumheller** views behavioral objectives as basic "navigational tools" for the educator. He points out that behavioral objectives are most effective when structured in terms of both "global" and "component" behaviors. Drumheller also indicates, within these two categories, that behavioral objectives should reflect several levels of comprehensiveness and specificity so as to match comfortably the varying predilections of an institution's staff. He discusses three types of climate that exist in public educational institutions—"political" climate, "school-playing" climate and the critically important but often ignored "educational" climate. He then illustrates the potential of global objectives for structuring and improving educational climate.

**Houston and Warner** trace the development of competency-based education from its origins as a specific conceptual entity less than ten years ago to its present stage of substantial educational and political influence. It is more than a coincidence, of course, that this decade of rapid growth in competency-based programs occurred simultaneously with a decade in which the use of behavioral objectives in various school settings also increased. Many types of competency-based programs were fostered by the behavioral objectives mind set, in which explicit objectives related to doing rather than just to knowing were paramount. The authors point out, for example, that competency-based teacher education grew directly out of the use of behavioral objectives for describing teacher effectiveness. They discuss the extensiveness of the competency-based movement, the primary problems that have surfaced, and the promise that such programs offer for the future.

**Niedermeyer and Sullivan** make the obvious association between the behavioral objectives movement and the current emergence, adoption and implementation of comprehensive objectives-based instructional programs. However, just as behavioral objectives were roundly criticized (and strongly defended) in the 1960s, so validated objectives-based instructional programs are now the target. The fact that the target *has* changed, however, is an interesting measure of the substantial acceptability that instructional objectives have achieved over the past decade. In Niedermeyer and Sullivan's view, the eventual outcome of current discussions concerning objectives-based programs will depend largely on pressures for accountability and on the help received by schools from specialized agencies and skilled instructional designers.

**Piper** seeks to build a workable and fruitful relationship between behavioral objectives and behavior modification. He has approached this task in a logical way and the result is a double-barreled effort at improving learning environments. Writing from a background in special education, he has broadened his comments to include the entire range of student abilities and instructional levels. Piper presents the familiar Magerian formula for behavioral objectives as well as basic behavior modification terminology and techniques. Piper also provides a useful analysis over time of the impact of behavioral approaches on several facets of schooling, including teacher evaluation, individualized instruction, and record-keeping systems.

**Harrow** writes from the perspective of a comprehensive background in physical education and movement education, having authored *A Taxonomy of the Psychomotor Domain: A Guide for Developing Behavioral Objectives*. In the present chapter, Harrow assesses the impact during recent years of behavioral objectives on the broad field of physical education. In proposing a framework for curriculum design and teacher education in the future, Harrow sees a need to constantly balance systematic and scientific approaches with creative and humanistic thrusts. In this task, she sees behavioral objectives as playing a significant role in fostering within each individual student the "ultimate athlete."

**Williams** describes the development and potential use of a behavioral "typology" of educational objectives in the cognitive domain. He acknowledges both the historical and functional influence of the well-known *Bloom Taxonomy of Educational Objectives* on the new typology. Williams points out, however, that the typology is a classification scheme for types of *tasks* rather than for types of *intellectual processes* required by various tasks, a factor that appears to promote ease and accuracy of use by teachers and instructional designers and to expose a range of cognitive abilities for instructional attention.

## Summary

Possible generalizations from the material just reviewed include the following:

(1)   Behavioral objectives represent one tool for systematic instructional design and validation.

(2)   Behavioral objectives represent a significant step toward a more scientific approach to teaching and learning.

(3)   Behavioral objectives may be written at a variety of levels of inclusiveness to serve the varying needs of educational decision makers, planners, implementers, and learners.

(4)   Highly specific behavioral objectives may be made meaningful by relating them to some type of variously labeled broader goals.

(5)   Behavioral objectives as a structural component of curriculum may be used either to free and expand learning environments or to control and limit them.

(6)   Behavioral objectives techniques may be shaped to meet emerging educational needs.

In summary, this book does not celebrate the end of a trend. Rather, it seeks to positively redirect the energy generated by the behavioral objectives movement toward varied solutions of challenging new problems and recurring old ones so that future educational programs can function more effectively.

M.B.K.

# Table of Contents

# BEHAVIORAL OBJECTIVES
## The Position of
## the Pendulum

# 1.
# The Nature and Role of Objectives in Instruction

Paul L. Dressel

Attempts to define the interests and aspirations of individuals and institutions are complicated by a prolific and confused terminology. Aims, goals, objectives and purposes are variously and hence obscurely used. Preferred processes (lectures, formally-structured and rigidly-scheduled classes), specific materials or authors (a particular textbook, Chaucer) and disciplinary requirements (literature, mathematics, foreign language, physical education) are so confused with objectives that the questioning of processes, materials or requirements may be interpreted as an attack on objectives or even on the competency and integrity of the teaching staff. In addition, the range of considerations or factors involved in national, regional, local and classroom educational planning ensures that proliferation and confusion of terminology will continue.

## Academic Discipline Goals

Teachers educated in one or more disciplines often view their task as that of presenting the disciplines to students who, in turn, are expected to master the terminology, principles and skills involved. The objectives may be unstated, being implicit in the tasks assigned and the tests given. Some teachers may look beyond the context or organized body of knowledge embraced by the discipline to the discipline as a mode of inquiry—a way to acquire and apply knowledge or to understand and cope with people,

3

problems and surroundings. These disciplinary-based behaviors, however, tend to be specific to the content covered, the tasks assigned and the tests given. Such objectives are so evident to teachers that insistence on specifying objectives seems to them to be inane and irrelevant.

### Life Related Goals

Educational philosophers and statesmen are not satisfied with this narrow disciplinary orientation and assert that broader, more integrated objectives having definitive relationships to life behavior are desirable. Some persons prefer emphasis on personal development and others on adaptive (if not entirely conforming) and productive behavior as a member of society. In the personal development conception, each individual establishes personal goals and means of achieving them which recognize the rights of others, both as individuals and as common users of the environment supporting all. Although priority is given to personal development, this must be within the context of society and of environmental resources. Individuals educated with this emphasis may be sensitized to the ills of society and undertake to remedy them. On the other hand, if priority is given to meeting societal needs and educating individuals to take their place in society and contribute to it, the objectives will reflect this orientation. The educational experience will encourage constructive conformity rather than idiosyncratic individuality.

Any attempt to promote objectives beyond disciplinary-based knowledge and methodological competency, especially at the college level, is handicapped by the disciplinary orientation of teachers. Teachers also have personal objectives and predilections, some of which are unverbalized and may even be unrecognized. Presenting the discipline is a far less demanding task, both in time and in ego involvement, than developing or socializing the individual. In an era when some teacher union contracts specify teaching contact hours and number of faculty meetings per semester, it cannot be assumed that faculty members will accept objectives which require more time and effort. Moreover, many college and university teachers are not especially interested in or adept at dealing with youth. Indeed some, though competent in their discipline, are not themselves good examples of adequate personal or social development. Educational institutions cannot be expected to foster in students objectives which the faculties and administrators do not exemplify.

**Student Goals**

Students, too, have objectives, but these objectives are not always explicit nor are they necessarily consonant with the roles of educational institutions or the competencies of teaching staffs. To assert that the student should state his or her own objectives is not altogether realistic, and it does not absolve teachers from stating objectives. Indeed, even the expectation that the individual student state personal objectives becomes a school or teacher objective. And the difficulty or complete inability of many students in this regard then requires a consideration of what educational experiences are required to bring the student to that point. With the student whose only goals are to acquire a motorcycle or car or to avoid work, the efforts (if any are made) of most teachers will probably be misdirected and unsuccessful. Clearly, affective characteristics (motivations, attitudes, and values) underlie educational objectives. Thus, the real issue is not between objectives being suggested or imposed by teachers and objectives being developed by individuals; it is in the relevance of the objectives to the individual and extent to which objectives (whatever their origin) are understood and accepted as personal goals.

Likewise, the educational experiences required to develop the resources, capabilities, and insights to attain an individual's objectives need not be developed by that individual. The patient who consults a physician does not make the diagnosis nor prognosis nor write the prescription. But the relevance and probable worth of consultation with a physician must be accepted eventually, and the prescribed regimen must be pursued with diligence if results are to be achieved. Individuals may also progress in respect to objectives that they neither recognize nor accept, but it is simply not sound education in a democracy to develop education so that it subtly indoctrinates. Moreover, conscious pursuit of objectives through developmental experiences recognized as relevant will achieve better results.

## Trend Toward Behavioral Objectives

Concern for providing experiences which promote individual development in regard to specific objectives, and the desire to determine (measure) the extent of growth, development, or change have led some educators to insist that objectives should be presented in behavioral form. This concept of behavioral objectives represents a recent attempt to state educational objectives in sufficiently specific terms (1) that the planning of educational experiences proceeds directly out of the statement of objectives, and (2) that the performance of the individual can be observed and evaluated. The concept is not really new. The concept of operational definition, developed in science some years ago to eliminate hypothetical concepts by defining a concept in terms of the steps or operations whereby the physical reality of that concept could be observed or measured, led to operational objectives which defined the performance intended so that it would be observable and evaluatable. Thus the words "operational," "performance," and "evaluatable" may, in some respects, be equated with "behavioral." Obviously, they are in stark contrast with complex global objectives such as critical thinking, citizenship, internalization of certain values, and mental and physical health, which have very little to do with day-to-day activities and are difficult to evaluate.

Since the behavior of individuals is to be observed and appraised, many proponents of behavioral objectives believe that criterion-referencing rather than norm-referencing of performance is desirable. Rather than a static comparison of individual performance with that of other individuals, in criterion-referenced evaluation a dynamic comparison of individual performance to an acceptable standard is made. This comparison would be accompanied by an indication of further work needed to reach any given standard. Mastery at a defined level (not perfection), rather than comparative adequacy, would be demanded.

In writing behavioral objectives, emphasis has been placed on the details of the behavior, the conditions under which it is to be performed, and on the production of a tangible product which can be observed and evaluated. The level of criteria of acceptable performance for an individual or class is also stated. An example of an objective phrased to meet this requirement is the following:

> The student will write a 300-500 word essay regarding his perception of the relationship of this course to his or her vocational and life goals.

To complete the specifications, the time, circumstances, and resources available should be stated. The minimal acceptable performance would be stated, including such factors as spelling, grammar, punctuation, content, adequacy of the student's grasp of the course, and its relevance to his goals. The teacher might also impose a personal accountability standard by indicating that 90 percent of the class will meet this requirement (Dressel, 1976).

### Covert and Overt Behavior

There are many and severe difficulties with this rigorous approach to defining behavioral objectives. Nonverbal mental processes are proscribed because there is no observable product, thus eliminating thought, judgment, feeling, creating, and synthesizing, except as these are ultimately verbalized or revealed by an observable product. These broad goals do represent a type of behavior but, being internal, it is not observable, and it may not be fully nor objectively reported by the individual. There are also mental processes in which language concepts are not used. The difficulty of an artist in expressing in words what he accomplished or tried to accomplish in a painting is indicative. Verbalizations about his work sound artificial and contrived. If the mental processes are language-based, individuals can accurately report some thought processes and, to some extent, the processes can be inferred from the results. The limitation of behavioral objectives to those which are observable essentially eliminates the broad, complex, and cumulative objectives—the truly important educational outcomes—and would replace them by specifics which are somewhat more performance oriented, but little better than the rote memorization of content and the purely verbal responses which still characterize so much of education at all ages and grades.

If broad, complex, integrative objectives are ignored in statements of objectives, they also are likely to be ignored in learning and in evaluation. In fact, by demanding that objectives specify overt behavior and thereby simultaneously ignoring covert mental processes, it is quite likely that erroneous judgments are made about student performance. Overt, observable behavior may be calculated to deceive. Even if it is not, the interpretation may be in error. The behavior observed may proceed out of covert mental processes and values other than what the observer assumes. The student writing an essay on the relationship of a course to his vocational and life goals knows that the essay will be read and evaluated by his instructor. Therefore, he is unlikely to assert that the course was without value or that he developed a dislike of the field because of his experience with it in the course. His deception may be as much a concern about injuring the ego of his instructor as for attaining a good grade.

### The Affective Component of Behavior

Objectives in the affective realm are especially difficult to state in behavioral terms, and the behavior (as the previous examples suggest) may be even more difficult to interpret. An instructor in a fine arts or humanities course might reasonably state that an anticipated behavioral outcome would be increased interest in and appreciation of art, music, or literature, as reflected in attendance at lectures, concerts, or art exhibits. Required attendance, enforced by examinations or the requirement of a critical report, reveals nothing about the objective. Completely optional attendance likewise provides no certain index of individual interest or preference, for some students may lack the money, have conflicting commitments, or have such demands from their courses that they cannot spare the time despite a desire to attend. The stating of overt, observable objectives does not solve the problems of giving direction to students or of providing incontrovertible evidence of progress. But the major weakness of dogmatic insistence of observability is that it results in a specificity which tends to make objectives "course bound." Such objectives may contribute to the fragmentation of experience and the isolation of courses by the emphasis on recall of specific content.

## Difficulty Levels of Tasks

In setting tasks whereby students exhibit the attainment of objectives, there must be a recognition of various levels of sophistication in responding to a single task as well as in responding to a series of increasingly difficult tasks. Faced with solving the quadratic equation, $X^2 - 5X + 6 = 0$, one student may, by trial-and-error, find the answers to be 2 and 3; another may solve it by factoring, and still another may see at once that the answers are 2 and 3 because these are the only two numbers whose product is 6 and whose sum is 5. There can be no doubt that the third student has greater insight (mastery, one might say), although the other two students also solved the problem. On the other hand, the sequence of equations

$$3X^2 - 5X - 50 = 0$$
$$3X^4 - 5X^2 - 50 = 50$$
$$3(2X - 7)^2 - 5(2X - 7) - 50 = 0$$
$$3A^{2n} - 5A^n - 50 = 0$$

will, for most students, present tasks of increasing conceptual as well as manipulative difficulty. But for the individual who has "fully grasped" the implication of a quadratic expression, the tasks are all essentially of the same difficulty. This individual might be said to have *mastered* the concept at a level implied by these tasks, although the truly knowledgeable person may reject the term "mastered" because the full meaning and implications of quadratic forms are certainly not even suggested by these recognition tasks.

These examples do indicate (though at a very simple conceptual level) that a major problem in stating objectives involving thought and judgmental processes is that there is a range of difficulty both in the processes and in the tasks to which the processes are applied. The validity of an argument may be demolished by an individual who knows and points out that one or more of the basic data items used is incorrect. Another individual may demonstrate that the logic is fallacious. The second would appear to be a more "difficult" task, although either criticism destroys the argument. And the individual who recognized both deficiencies can be devastating in his comments.

An individual who plots on coordinate paper paired values of two variables and notes that the resulting points approximate a straight line may lack the awareness of or the ability to use covariance or regression analysis. An elementary school student might do the first, but he or she is unlikely to be able to do the second because the methodology is not usually taught prior to the college level, and most elementary school students could not understand or apply it. Clearly, individuals may differ in mental ability, in knowledge, facts, concepts, and principles, and in knowledge and ability to use analytic tools and modes of inquiry. Formal education makes only limited acknowledgment of these differences except in those disciplines which are cumulative and in which there exists a sequence of courses, each depending upon those preceding it in the sequence. And even here, the stated (or possibly implicit and unstated) objectives tend to be so highly specific to the course as to fail to suggest longer term and broader competencies.

## Long-Term Objectives

Nowhere is this failure to state and plan education on the basis of long-term objectives more apparent than in discussions of liberal education in colleges and universities. With few exceptions, the pragmatic definition of liberal education is in distribution or course requirements. Because of the disciplinary orientation of the faculty, liberal education is defined by an enforced contact with the liberal arts which are diversely defined and valued. If, in contrast, liberal education were defined by the following six competencies, liberal education would still seem more than a series of courses. It would also seem not clearly separable from vocational education, as the competencies are equally applicable there. Most educators will agree that the liberally educated individual should:

(1) be aware of his or her abilities and utilize them effectively;
(2) have a high level of mastery of communication skills;
(3) have a consciousness of his or her own values and value commitments and an understanding of the values of others;
(4) relate himself effectively to others and find self-realization and self-expression by so doing;
(5) relate his or her knowledge and values to the contemporary scene; and
(6) have a concern for and the ability to organize and interrelate or integrate knowledge, abilities, and values.

A graduate who succeeds to a reasonable measure in attaining these goals will not only have attained a liberal education, but will also be able to earn a living in many fields and to continue his education, whether or not he chooses to pursue additional formal education in a professional or graduate school.

These competencies, to be effective guides to educational planning, must be elaborated somewhat. The following discussion (Dressel, 1971) will attempt to do this. Each competency is *clarified* by defining the key words in its statement. The *range of application* is indicated. Examples of *relevant learning experiences* are provided and *possible evidences of accomplishment* are noted. By this analysis, each competency emerges as descriptive of widely applicable behavior, suggestive of appropriate learning experiences, and readily evaluatable by some form of observation and record.

*Competency 1.    The student should know how to acquire knowl-
                  edge and how to use it.*

"To acquire knowledge" includes collection and evaluation of
source material, interviews, firsthand observation, interpretation
of data, and experimentation. "How to use it" includes evaluation
of accuracy and relevance, application, explanation, mediation,
and analysis of possible courses of action. This competency applies
to problems in all areas of activity (vocational, social, personal).
Relevant learning experiences include independent study, community service, team learning, study of current problems, special
projects, and written and oral expression. The learning experiences
provided should provide for assessment of the competency
through observation of the process or analyses of the performance
(paper, laboratory report, art object, etc.).

This assessment involves three levels: determination of whether
and to what extent individuals have had experiences appropriate
to the development of the competency, study of each such
experience to see if it actually requires and contributes to the
development of the competency, and assessment of individual
competency. The assessment of individual competency requires a
clear definition of what is involved in the competency. For
example, an independent study project report may be read to
determine use of sources, observation, and experimentation. It
may also be read to determine how the knowledge gained was
applied. If the learning experiences are too limited or yield no
objective evidence of performance, comprehensive assessment may
require additional tasks which provide further evidence of competency. A senior thesis or a senior independent study project
might provide a significant part of the evidence required.

*Competency 2.    The student should have a high level of mastery
                  of the skills of communication.*

"High level of mastery" includes such items as perceptiveness in
acquiring information and assessing attitudes, accuracy in using
technical vocabulary, facility with the grammar of the discipline,

adaptability to audiences, flexibility in style, and cogency in criticism. "Skills of communication" include reading with facility of both popular and scholarly materials, listening in formal and informal situations, speaking to large assemblies and small groups, and writing formal research papers and critical essays. This competency applies to problems centering around communication associated with nonacademic and vocational activity as well as with the academic program. Relevant learning experiences include reading (analysis and evaluation of newspapers, magazines, and scholarly or research papers), listening (lectures, interviewing, and small group discussions), speaking (reading a formal paper, class recitations, small group discussions, debates and dramatics), and writing (technical reports, classroom papers, critical analysis).

Since a student almost constantly communicates with himself or others by reading, listening, speaking, or writing, evidence of accomplishment may be collected at various times under many different conditions. The following questions are appropriate: (1) How many significant points does a student recall from a lecture just heard? (2) How accurate are the data obtained from observation or from an interview? (3) How reliable are student perceptions of phenomena or of the attitudes and views of his associates? (4) How well organized and how clear is the student's formal expression? The conditions of each observation should be noted, and these limitations may require that additional observations be made. Communication patterns are important not only in revealing the quality and amount of communication, but in providing evidence on the other five competencies which can be observed and assessed only as the student communicates them by word or action.

*Competency 3.* *The student should be aware of his own values and value commitments and realize that other individuals and cultures hold contrasting values which must be understood and, to some extent, accepted in interaction with them.*

This statement assumes that most individuals have a set of values, although they may curry favor or avoid difficulty by appearing to accept the values of others. But individuals are not always conscious of their values. The valuing behavior may have been assimilated without recognition or it may have become habitual. The statement also assumes that values are largely culturally determined, that there are no absolutes, and that meaningful interactions among people require understanding and acceptance rather than mere tolerance.

"Being aware of something" means being conscious of and sufficiently concerned to be willing to attend to it. "Values" connote those considerations or points of view (conscious or unconscious) which are given priority through choice or action when differing values yield differing choices. "Understood" means that the contrasting values are known and recognized as contrasting. The implications of these contrasting values are sensed—at least in part—and the origin or justification for them understood. "Accepted" means that such contrasting values are not automatically rejected as untenable or wrong because they are different. Respect is accorded to the culture in which these values are imbedded, although the values themselves may be regarded as unacceptable. "Interaction" includes situations (communication, cooperation, confrontation) in which the individual does or does not exhibit sympathetic and rational treatment of the views, customs, and actions of individuals with contrasting values.

This competency applies to all activities of an individual. Although individuals should not become so self-conscious and introspective as to become incapable of action, circumstances often generate views, attitudes, or behavior without conscious attention to the values supported. Social mores and personal habits are often efficient behavior determinants in that they may allow time for more significant thought and pursuit of deeper meanings. Yet the life unexamined in detail may not be examined at all. Recognition of value differences readily leads to the valuing of originality and creativity which, along with critical inquiry, are basic value commitments of higher education.

Any experience (in or out of class, on or off campus) can promote value sensitivity if individuals consciously address the reasons for their views and actions. But some experiences have more potential than others because they reveal values so different that they cannot be ignored. Differences in speech, food, dress, esthetic standards, use of leisure time, politics, and religion, even among students from various parts of the same country, can provide the initial stimulation for value analysis. At times, probing into the rationale for one's own views and those of other students and professors may be required. Some individuals may require a "culture shock," such as is attainable only by attempting to live in a community of a very different pattern from that to which they have been accustomed. Although courses and other structured experiences make some contribution to value consciousness and motivation analysis, experiences such as community service, team learning, and study abroad may be more effective.

The learning experiences should include assessment of competency development through observation of the process or analysis of the result (paper, laboratory report, art object, etc.). The assessment should include the extent to which individuals have become aware of their values, of the value differences and conflicts among their immediate associates, and of cultures with greatly contrasting values. The assessment should also undertake to determine the consistency of actions and values, the ability to use values in understanding the views and behavior of others, willingness to be exposed to value differences, and concern for and recognition of originality and creativity. This evaluation should be formative in nature, providing feedback as necessary.

*Competency 4.   The student should be able to cooperate and collaborate with others in studying, analyzing, and formulating solutions to problems and in taking action on them.*

The first of the preceding competencies emphasizes the ability to acquire and apply knowledge. It does not bar the assistance of or collaboration with others; it simply demands that each individual possess competency in some measure. This fourth competency insists that the individual also be able to cooperate and collaborate with others. The very nature of a democratic society and its associated technology demands that individuals relate themselves effectively to others and find self-realization rather than self-obliteration in so doing. This competency obviously involves the second competency (communication) and the third (values). Effective communication is a prelude to cooperation and collaboration. Effective cooperation and collaboration also depend upon valuing the individuality and creativity of each individual.

"Cooperate" and "collaborate" are both used in the statement of this competency in the belief that collaboration involves more acceptance of the worth of group effort than does mere cooperation which may be little more than acceptance of the ideas and efforts of others. "Study" suggests acquiring knowledge by systematic investigation. "Analysis" involves not only the separation of the problem itself into its constitutent elements (assumptions, factors, and possible causes), but also the recognition of opinions, relevant facts, materials, and principles useful in solving the problem. "Action" has a wide range of meanings, depending upon the nature of the problem and the range of persons or factors involved in it. If a problem concerns only the members of the team investigating it, the necessary actions may emerge almost immediately from the tentative solution. If the problem involves others, persuading the larger group to accept the solution may be difficult.

This competency applies to problems in every aspect of life. Relevant learning experiences include team or group projects and reports, committee assignments, community service projects, seminars involving divisions of responsibility in studying and analyzing a problem, and community surveys. The learning experiences should include assessment of the competency through observation of the process and analysis of the result. The result is a composite of the work of several individuals. The extent and nature of a single individual's collaboration, or whether and to what extent individuals have had experiences appropriate to the development of the competency, may not be easily determined. It is also desirable to study student participation and ascertain that it actually uses and strengthens the competency. Observation, self-appraisal, and group appraisal of the extent to which individuals contribute substantially and dynamically to the group effort will be appropriate.

A primary concern with this competency involves the individual's ability to facilitate group deliberation, task allotment, and synthesis of the individual skills involved to accomplish a task which could not be performed by individuals or would be done less efficiently or effectively by them.

*Competency 5.   The student should have an awareness of, concern for, and sense of responsibility about contemporary events, issues, and problems.*

"Awareness," "concern," and "sense of responsibility" suggest successive and cumulative levels of attention. "Awareness" simply indicates knowledge that certain issues or problems exist. "Concern" implies direction of attention to these events and some degree of anxiety about the implications or outcomes. "Sense of responsibility" involves some personal obligation for considering the implications of events and for helping to resolve issues or solve problems.

No one can be aware of all events, but the educated person must address those having significant implications for society and his role in it. Politics, sports, catastrophes, and medical science are all relevant. Some issues are timeless, but events generate new issues or new aspects of issues. For example, what are the moral and legal implications of human organ removal and replacement? The problems themselves may be current (open housing legislation) or timeless (equality and justice for all). Awareness, concern, and responsibility are seldom inculcated by learning experiences developed and directed to those ends, although this is not impossible. Rather, they result from projection of a program or college image that attracts students more concerned with problems than with mastery of a discipline; from a faculty that demonstrates, in and out of class, that it is vitally concerned about life.

Almost any learning experience can provide opportunity for development of this competency if that development becomes a continuing and conscious concern of the student. For example, group discussions of contemporary issues encourage students to express their concerns and permit them to examine the implications of these issues personally as well as socially. The nature of the relevant experiences suggests that evaluation of accomplishment may have to depend largely on observation and subjective appraisal. Tests on contemporary affairs or current events will indicate awareness, but they do not demonstrate concern and responsibility. This competency is related to the preceding ones. Concern and responsibility are evidenced when students acquire and use knowledge about an event, issue, or problem, when they develop and exchange views with others, when they cooperate and collaborate with others in study and action, and when they identify the values implicit in various views and relate these values to their own. The fifth competency requires that the competencies be related to the contemporary scene.

Evidence of accomplishment is sought by appraising the extent to which the program promotes attention (in class and out) to contemporary events, issues, and problems; by determining the extent of students' spontaneous participation in communications and actions about issues and problems; and by determining the extent to which individuals exhibit awareness and concern and take some responsibility for formulating a personal point of view and for action on some issue or problem.

*Competency 6.    The student should be able to relate his development of competencies into a coherent, cumulative, and somehow unified college experience and to apply these competencies to his further development as an individual and to fulfillment of his obligation as a responsible citizen in a democratic society.*

The length, the concepts used, and the relation of this competency to the preceding competencies suggest that it is a complex capstone competency. Its significance lies in its integrative implications. "Coherent" implies cohesiveness, consistency, interrelatedness, and connectedness. It emphasizes that experiences planned by the college are congruous with each other and mutually complementary. "Cumulative" means that early experiences provide the foundation for later experiences and that the latter simultaneously build upon and bind together the earlier experiences to achieve new levels of insight and competency. "Somehow unified" suggests that the desired unity or integration is largely an individual accomplishment, neither fully predictable nor *a priori* describable.

This competency expresses the purpose that the individual find a sense of accomplishment and satisfaction in progressive increase in competencies, viewed as ever more relevant both to scholarship and to life. The resulting unity, peculiar to the individual, provides self-confidence for the work ahead. This competency must be a concern in each and every aspect of the student's experience. This experience must be examined both retrospectively and especially prospectively if the student is to sense progress and find an essential unity in that cumulative experience. Incongruence and inconsistency become a challenge to seek coherence rather than a confusing and disheartening discontinuity.

Periodic student self-evaluation assists in organizing such experiences and assessing their impact. Advisers and teachers can assist in this process. Such self-evaluation should be so conducted as to encourage planning and selection of experiences which contribute to further development. The involvement of students in evaluating college impact will also focus attention on this competency. The student who raises questions about relationships between current studies and past ones or who attempts to apply acquired knowledge to current problems is attempting to exercise this competency. Conversations, papers, and actions can be reviewed to determine the extent to which a wide range of relevant ideas or concepts is brought to bear on a problem and the extent to which there is awareness of the values involved in the problem.

Some such statement of competencies and an analysis of conditions producing them are essential if a sense of cumulative growth and unity is to be fostered by the curriculum. The competencies are so interrelated that the experiences appropriate to foster one of them may very likely be appropriate for others.

### Values Education

Since competency in valuing, which obviously transcends courses and content, offers special problems in defining sequence, some discussion (Dressel, 1966) of it will illustrate the task of planning experiences directed to personal development over time. College students are never value free. They often rebel against values, as interpreted and enforced by adults, which have a rationale but are dimly understood by youth. But the college student may be a prisoner of values unrecognized because no crisis has yet brought awareness of them. Uniformity in dress and behavior and lackadaisical scholastic performance exemplify such conformity. Each student, in reference to values and insight into and commitment to them, is already an individual. Yet some sequence of steps by which an individual progresses in greater insight and commitment is necessary.

A value-oriented instructional program begins by provoking the student to awareness of personal values. This includes an awareness of the extent to which his decisions and actions have been value based (perhaps largely unconsciously), and an awareness also of the consistency of professed values with decisions and actions.

The student also develops an awareness of the values of associates and of the culture. The student benefits from realizing that his own views and behavior are often predicated on values quite different from those of his associates. The student will also benefit from a realization that agreement on major issues and actions is sometimes possible despite disagreements.

Value sensitivity is greately enhanced when placed in contact with markedly different value systems. Contacts with foreign students on campus or foreign travel help to accomplish this, as do readings, films, television, and foreign visitors. A significant element in these contacts is the realization that the appropriateness and even the existence of certain values must be examined in reference to the social context. A natural extension of this awareness of cultures of other groups and societies is the projection of identified value positions into later periods than those in which they were generally accepted. Thus colonialism was based on identifiable values and on attitudes toward "inferior" races. This syndrome has unfortunate consequences in the present day. Educated estimates of ultimate consequences, uncertain though they be, often furnish the only rational grounds for choice among courses of action.

At some point, students should reassess and possibly revise or restructure their personal values. Having become aware of their own values, having seen the similarities and differences between their values and those of both close associates and of other human beings more remote in time and space, the individual should be ready for personal value review and reevaluation.

The ordering of these four steps or stages is more psychological than logical. They appear here to be rather more separable than will be found in actual practice. For particular individuals or values, even the sequence of the four steps may alter. Nevertheless, this sequential structure provides some basis for planning both for a group of students over three or four years and for individuals in that group.

## Summary
The competency objectives discussed in this article transcend courses, but courses and disciplines can contribute to the

development of the competencies. If not behavioral in the strictest sense of behavioral objectives, they are, nevertheless, objectives which affect behavior, and much of that behavior is observable. These competency objectives suggest the educational experiences necessary to promote them. The range of situations where the competencies are relevant includes many levels of difficulty and can involve ideas and modes of inquiry from all disciplines. The individual who attains them will not necessarily be happier or a better citizen. But at the least he will be capable of leading a more effective and rewarding life and of contributing to the improvement of society. And this, after all, is exactly what education is supposed to do. Education can be effective in these regards only if every teacher and every educational experience is viewed and developed in reference to its potential for promoting progress toward these objectives.

## References

Dressel, P.L. *College and University Curriculum.* Berkeley, California: McCutchan Publishing Corporation, 1971, 285-297.

Dressel, P.L. *Handbook of Academic Evaluation.* San Francisco, California: Jossey-Bass Publishers, 1976, 45-48.

Dressel, P.L. Value-Oriented Instructional Techniques. *Improving College and University Teaching,* Summer 1966, *14,* 138-144.

# 2.
# Expanding Behavioral Objectives for Educational Design

Philip G. Kapfer

Physical and biological scientists are accustomed to dealing both with what can and what cannot be seen. Although no one has directly observed individual oxygen or nitrogen molecules, which are the principal components of air, scientists deal with air in multitudes of ways. Thus, even though air cannot be seen, it would be counter-productive to say, "Air does not exist." Rather, scientists predict certain indicators—the observable and measurable effects of air—for testing their hypotheses concerning the existence and nature of air. For example, the diffusion of smoke particles throughout an enclosed container can be attributed to the bombardment of unobservable air molecules. The presence, *per se*, of the air molecules is not proven by such experiments but, rather, the *properties* of such molecules (and, therefore, their presence) become increasingly known. To modify the familiar saying somewhat, "Where there's diffusion, there's air."

The covert mental behaviors of people are like air molecules in that they are unobservable by direct means and must be "smoked out" by indirect methods. You cannot see another person's concept, but you know it is there by a variety of indicators. For example, the different responses of several people to the same stimulus can be attributed to the mediating influence of each person's own unique but invisible concepts and feelings.

Strict "behaviorists" have strongly influenced the behavioral objectives movement to ignore covert behaviors. For example, while discussing the nature of behavioral objectives, Gage and Berliner (1975) stated, "Educators and especially educational psychologists have increasingly adopted the principle that objectives [for teaching] should be stated in terms of observable behaviors of students" (p. 39). The adoption of this principle for curricular and instructional design and for the development of evaluation strategies is an unnecessary limitation (Woodruff and Kapfer, 1972). A fundamental cause of the problem is that there has not been a good mechanism for dealing simultaneously with both covert and overt behavior.

The purpose of this chapter is to present a definition of behavior that lends itself to analyzing both the covert and overt elements of behavior, both separately and in combination. We will then demonstrate the manner in which this definition contributes to (1) curriculum development (i.e., content identification), (2) instructional design (i.e., teaching-learning activities), and (3) evaluation design. In other words, we will look at methods of dealing with the overt "smoke signals" that allow educators to expose the properties of covert behavior.

**Behavior Defined**

As mentioned, behavior often has been defined as a visible action or act. A possible first step in redefining behavior is to agree that invisible mental actions are the basis for voluntary visible behaviors and that ways need to be found to deal with such covert behaviors in a practical manner. Therefore, in our definition of behavior, the word "act" will refer *both to visible or overt acts and to mental or covert acts.*

Secondly, we will assume in defining behavior that no one performs a covert or overt act without doing it to or on something. Therefore, behavior is an "act" upon something where the "something" could be a real thing or a memory of a real thing. The "somethings" that we act upon are "phenomena" (i.e., objects and events). Thus, a somewhat more concise statement of our definition of behavior as developed thus far is "an act upon a phenomenon."

Common sense tells us that it is rather difficult to "act upon a phenomenon" without causing something else to happen. "Consequence" is an appropriate word to connote all of the results of our acts upon phenomena. Thus our completed definition of behavior is as follows: *Behavior is an ACT upon a PHENOMENON that results in a CONSEQUENCE* (Kapfer, Kapfer, and Woodruff, 1976). This definition is presented as an equation in Figure 1.

Before demonstrating the use of this definition in curricular, instructional and evaluation design, we will look at examples of behavior involving covert and overt "acts" to show how this definition of behavior may be employed. In Figure 2, using the new definition of behavior and using "flame test" as the phenomenon, a possible sequence of behavior involving concept formation is outlined. Behaviors involving overt actions also may be analyzed readily, as demonstrated in Figure 3.

An interesting consequence of analyzing behavior in this manner is that mixtures of observable and non-observable components frequently can be identified and dealt with in educational situations. For example, in the first behavior listed in Figure 2, the act (seeing) and the consequence (a mental image stored in the student's mind as a memory of the perceptual experience) are not observable by any direct means, whereas the phenomenon (flame test) is of course directly observable. It is apparent from Figures 2 and 3 that both covert (e.g., recalling) and overt (e.g., chloride testing) actions are required for the chemistry student to function effectively. The new definition of behavior allows for the identification of both.

*Figure 1*

*Definition of Behavior*

Behavior = (Act + Phenomenon → Consequence)

*Figure 2*

*Examples of Behaviors Involving Covert Actions*

| ACT | + PHENOMENON | → CONSEQUENCE |
|---|---|---|
| (1) Seeing | + flame test of lithium compound | → percept (mental image) of crimson flame |
| (2) Thinking | + memories of flame tests of selected metallic compounds | → recalled mental images of various flame colors |
| (3) Recalling | + memories of common properties of flame tests of selected metallic compounds | → generalized mental construct (concept) of characteristic colors imparted to flames during flame tests of selected metallic compounds |

*Figure 3*

*Examples of Behaviors Involving Overt Actions*

| ACT | + PHENOMENON | → CONSEQUENCE |
|---|---|---|
| (1) Identifying | + KCl | → name (potassium chloride) |
| (2) Flame testing | + KCl | → magenta color that potassium characteristically imparts to flame |
| (3) Chloride testing | + KCl | → white precipitate of AgCl |

## Curriculum Design Using "Phenomena"

Curriculum design refers to identifying subject matter. When developing the new definition of behavior, we said that every "act" is performed upon something—and we named the something a "phenomenon." The following question now can be asked. When identifying the curricular content for a course of study, will the name of the phenomenon usefully stand in the place of an analysis of behaviors or a list of behavioral objectives? Based on our curriculum development work in kindergarten through twelfth grade general education, in teacher education and in medical education, the answer would seem to be yes. This phenomena-based approach to the identification of curricular content has the distinct advantage of being briefer than the more familiar verbal concept statements and behavioral objectives approach to the same task. For example, Figure 4 contains the names of phenomena that could be combined into a course at any one of several levels of difficulty and inclusiveness.* When a specific behavior involving a particular phenomenon is needed for such a course, appropriate "actions" and "consequences" may be added to the phenomenon so that a behavior is fully identified. The "actions" and "consequences" that are added will depend on the purposes, backgrounds, and academic levels of the specific students involved. The behaviors identified by this means then may become teacher/learner objectives.

## Instructional Design Using "Phenomena"

Instructional design refers to the organization of teaching and learning. In this section, alternatives will be examined for putting

---

*The curriculum development process used in Figure 4 is described and illustrated by Woodruff and Kapfer (1973). Briefly, the process involves *generation* followed by *analysis*. In Figure 4, the generation process of working through increasingly specific categories of phenomena is illustrated to the point at which single "whole things" (in this case, a set of photographic prints to be entered in an exhibit) can be identified. From that point onward, the analysis process is employed for identifying components of any such "whole things."

*Figure 4*

*Phenomena as Curricular Content*

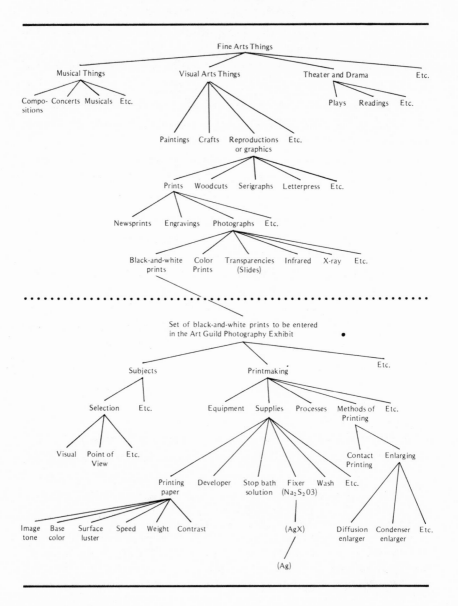

phenomena into behavioral form using several instructional designs. A possible classification scheme for the instructional designs might be the following:

(1)   Open-ended inquiry ("want-to-know" learning)
(2)   Focused inquiry ("need-to-know" learning)
(3)   Issue resolution (goal choosing)
(4)   Production ("product" making)

The relationship between these four instructional designs and the phenomena-based approach to curriculum development just discussed can be illustrated by an example. Using the curriculum content in Figure 4, and arranging a portion of it in linear form, we have the following 12 possible items of content:

(1)   Fine arts things
(2)   Visual arts things
(3)   Reproductions or graphics
(4)   Prints
(5)   Photographs
(6)   Black-and-white prints
(7)   Set of black-and-white prints for an exhibit
(8)   Printmaking
(9)   Supplies
(10)  Fixer: sodium thiosulfate ($Na_2S_2O_3$)
(11)  Silver halide ($AgX + Na_2S_2O_3 \rightarrow$ soluable silver complexes)
(12)  Silver ($AgX + \bar{e} \rightarrow Ag + X^-$)

Relating these items of content and the first instructional design identified above, it is evident that a student could "want" to know about any one of the items and therefore could engage in "open-ended" inquiry to satisfy that want. This kind of inquiry is classified as open-ended because the learning outcomes are defined by individual student curiosity rather than by the requirements of some task.

Turning now to the second instructional design, "focused" inquiry also could occur with respect to any of the curricular content items. This kind of inquiry receives its focus from a foreknowledge of the situation(s) in which the new learnings will be needed. This is what we mean by a "need" to know. For example, the student needs to know the steps in the printmaking process before he can produce a set of prints of sufficient quality to be entered in a photography exhibit. Sometimes the teacher's foreknowledge of the use of the curricular content in question is substituted for the student's (e.g., "You will need to know how to use various kinds of printing paper to obtain differing effects before engaging in print production"), but if this happens consistently, it may be an indication of inadequate instructional design.

It is apparent that "want-to-know" and "need-to-know" learning are distinguished not principally by content focus but by two other factors. First, in "want-to-know" learning, motivation is based on curiosity, while in "need-to-know" learning it is based on an actual use for the knowledge. Second, "want-to-know" learning may lead in virtually any direction, while "need-to-know" learning receives its focus from the anticipated use of the newly acquired competence.

Issue resolving, the third instructional design, also could incorporate any of the above curricular content items in at least two ways. First, any of these items could be the *central focus* of an issue. For example, "What should be done about photographic subjects for the Art Guild Exhibit?" Second, any of the items could become involved as *possible alternatives for resolving* an issue. For example, in an issue concerning the artistic effects to be obtained from the selection of alternative photographic subjects, the characteristics of the printing paper that is available will have an influence on the choices that may be made. Likewise, the accessibility of some type of enlarging equipment will bear directly on the student photographer's capability for removing detrimental features from an otherwise suitable photographic subject (and therefore on his choice of subject). In this brief example, a substantial variety of curricular content items from Figure 4 would be made available for student study within the context of real-life usage.

The fourth and final instructional design, "product" making, could focus on whatever concrete items are of interest or use to the learner. In general, "whole things," such as a specific set of photographs for the Art Guild Exhibit, are best capable of stimulating and sustaining a productive level of student work. Parts of whole things, such as contact printing, also may be sufficiently unitary to promote motivated production and learning.

Now that we have described four possible instructional designs that make use of phenomena, we can contrast the varying functions of behavioral objectives in these designs with the functions of behavioral objectives in conventional instructional designs that make use of concept statements. In conventional approaches, the learner typically is presented with verbal materials at a fairly rapid rate. These verbal materials contain the concept statements of the textbook author or the teacher. The learner frequently is asked to remember these verbalizations about objects or events whether or not he has had sufficient experience with them for them to be meaningful or of immediate practical use to him. In phenomena-based approaches to instruction, the learner has direct experience with real things *following which* he is expected to associate appropriate verbal labels and formulate statements of concepts and principles. The difference between these two approaches to instructional design is not the difference between deductive and inductive methods of teaching and learning. Both deductive and inductive methods may be used in both approaches to instructional design. Rather, the difference is experiential learning vs. primarily verbal learning through rote memorization. These comparisons are further clarified by means of a series of contrasting statements presented in Figure 5.

Thus, in phenomena-based instructional designs, behavioral objectives take the following general forms, which are made as specific as is needed for the purposes of communication within the designs themselves:

(1) For *open-ended inquiry*, the behavioral objective is to

*Figure 5*

*Contrasting the Nature and Role of Behavioral*
*Objectives in Two Types of Instructional Designs*

---

### Phenomena-Based Instructional Designs

1. Instructional design begins with the selection of a phenomenon.

2. The learner's purpose determines the instructional design.

3. The instructional design guides the learner to the overt and covert behaviors that match his or her purpose.

4. These behaviors (a) begin with experiential learning, (b) are followed immediately by words that name, describe, summarize, and organize that learning, and (c) may expand to include covert and overt actions that result in concrete want-serving and life-based products for which the experiential and verbal learnings are prerequisites.

5. Learner objectives follow logically from the above, and serve to facilitate evaluation design.

### Concept Statement-Based Instructional Designs

1. Instructional design begins with the selection of concept statements and corresponding behavioral objectives that specify overt learner actions.

2. The teacher's purpose determines the instructional design.

3. The instructional design guides the learner to the overt actions required by the behavioral objectives.

4. The overt actions are verbal or non-verbal and are often evaluation-serving products that may or may not relate directly to the in-life or on-the-job wants and needs of the learner.

5. Evaluation follows directly and is usually identical to or representative of the overt actions prescribed in the behavioral objectives originally selected.

---

become familiar with (know and understand something about) a given phenomenon and its properties.

(2)  For *focused inquiry*, the behavioral objective is to understand the functional properties of a phenomenon in order to use the phenomenon competently for some purpose.

(3)  For *issue resolution*, the behavioral objective is to choose a course of action and, therefore, a goal, and to do so in a rational fashion.

(4)  For *"product" making*, the behavioral objective is to build, produce, prepare, obtain, create, develop, etc., a product which meets established specifications or criteria.

To summarize the phenomena-based approach to instructional design, the following steps and outcomes are critical. *Phenomena* are *identified* and then *matched* to the appropriate *instructional designs*. This strategy may increase the probability that behavioral outcomes will be determined (1) by student wants and needs (positive motivational factors) and (2) by the natural laws that govern the phenomena being used (life-based environmental factors).

## Evaluation Design Using Overt and Covert Behaviors

Evaluation design refers to ways of measuring learning outcomes. By defining and analyzing behavior as described above, we may be able to do the following: (1) directly observe and measure overt components of behavior, and (2) increasingly expose the properties of covert components of behavior by observation and measurement of overt indicators of those properties. This might work as follows.

One example of a behavior is the following statement from Figure 2: "Seeing, plus a flame test of lithium compound, leads to the percept (mental image) of crimson flame." Overt indicators of the student's covert "seeing" might include (1) the student's eyes being turned in the direction of the flame test, and (2) his observational statements about the test. Overt indicators of the student's recognition or memory of the phenomenon might include (1) his being able to name, describe, identify or otherwise specify the equipment used to carry out the flame test, (2) his being able to reproduce the flame test given the necessary equipment, and (3) his being able to distinguish the flame test from other types of chemical tests. Overt indicators of the student's covertly developed "mental image" might include (1) his describing pictorially or verbally the crimson flame, (2) his identifying a lithium flame test from unlabeled colored pictures of sodium, potassium, lithium, barium, strontium, and calcium flame tests, and (3) his identifying a lithium compound from among three unlabeled salts when given the equipment necessary to conduct flame tests.

Data about each of these indicators may be gathered and analyzed in order to characterize the chemistry student's behavior. Such data concerning the student's behavior, both before and after instructional intervention, become evidence of the effectiveness of the intervention. An evaluator who is familiar with the details of the intervention should have little difficulty making these indicators operational for data collection purposes.

## Summary

Behavior has been defined in this chapter as "an act upon a phenomenon resulting in a consequence." A number of examples have been used to demonstrate the manner in which this definition may be applied to overt and covert components of behavior. The use of this definition of behavior has implications for the curriculum developer, the instructional designer and the evaluation specialist.

First, curriculum designers who find behavioral objectives to be a useful tool will no longer be forced to neglect the covert components of behavior. The type of behavioral objectives presented here contains a combination of overt and covert components. In addition, the process of identifying subject matter may be simplified because the focus will be on *phenomena* instead of on the actions people take with respect to phenomena.

Second, use of this definition of behavior will allow instructional designers to specify behavioral objectives based on in-life usage of phenomena rather than stating such objectives primarily for the purpose of meeting evaluation needs. Such life-based learning can be accomplished by matching subject matter (phenomena) to appropriate instructional designs, depending on the learner's purpose. Thus, for example, "focused" inquiry will receive its focus from the knowledge requirements for issue resolving or "product" making. Emergent learning will be fostered through the use of instructional designs in which the student defines his or her own behavioral objectives as an integral part of using open-ended inquiry processes.

Third, evaluation designers will be able to employ both direct and indirect measures of each of the three components of behavior. Such measures, when taken together, may provide more convincing evidence for learning than do the isolated "observable actions" that are evaluated using the conventional definition of behavior.

The future of behavioral objectives in education may be enhanced substantially through use of a total definition of behavior that more nearly matches reality. Scientists in other fields made analogous moves early in the history of their specialties. Air and percepts, photons and concepts, and numerous other covert phenomena surely challenge our ingenuity. Our task is to "smoke them out" through whatever indirect means the reality of their existence will allow.

## References

Gage, N.L. and D.C. Berliner. *Educational Psychology.* Chicago, Illinois: Rand McNally College Publishing Company, 1975.
Kapfer, P.G., M.B. Kapfer and A.D. Woodruff. Declining Test Scores:

Interpretations, Issues, and Relationship to Life-Based Education. *Educational Technology*, July 1976, *16*, 5-12.

Woodruff, A.D. and P.G. Kapfer. Behavioral Objectives and Humanism in Education: A Question of Specificity. *Educational Technology*, January 1972, *12*, 51-55.

Woodruff, A.D. and P.G. Kapfer. *A Life-Involvement Teacher Education Curriculum*. Salt Lake City, Utah: Bureau of Educational Research, University of Utah, 1973.

# 3.
# Conceptual Objectives for Domain-Referenced Education

## Philip W. Tiemann

What is behavioral about behavioral objectives? Even those of us who have worked with objectives for years would do well to consider this question. Michael MacDonald-Ross (1973), one of the trenchant critics of behavioral objectives, raised essentially this issue with the following observation:

> Philosophers often make the distinction between behaviours (movements or muscle twitches) and action (which must meet various *criteria*). This is what MacMillan and McClellan (1968) allude to when they say: "But the curious thing about the acceptable objectives is that they do not give descriptions of behaviour, but rather specify criteria of correctness of *results* of behaviour . . . the behavioural objectives, then, are not behavioural" (p. 32).

Elsewhere in his lengthy critique, MacDonald-Ross voiced approval of the distinction made by Mager (1961) between course descriptions (what the teacher does) and instructional objectives (what the student does). MacDonald-Ross also recognized that an emphasis upon what a student should *do*, as opposed to what a student should *know*, is a "sound and practically useful" distinction. As MacDonald-Ross observed, ". . . it has probably been the major contribution of behavioural objectives to the improvement of education and training, if only because the distinction encourages people to *think what they mean* when they plan a course" (p. 11).

The useful component of behavioral objectives, recognized even by their critics, is a focus upon student behavior rather than teacher behavior. Since both are behavior, it may be time to emphasize the obvious and insist that any instructional objective must describe *student* actions (to use the philosopher's term) or performances (in the behavioral sense).

## Descriptive Labeling

Neither Mager's first text (1961) nor his retitled version (1962), acknowledged by many as responsible for the current interest in behavioral objectives, made use of the adjective "behavioral." Mager referred to "clear" objectives and "meaningfully stated" objectives and, as contrasting instances, "poorly stated" objectives, but he did not introduce the term "behavioral objectives."

The term "behavioral" carries an unfortunate connotation, suggesting to critics that its advocates are not interested in student cognition, the "knowing" component of education. For instance, Waks (1969) refers to a behaviorist orientation as merely enabling students to answer examination questions in contrast to "understanding algebra." He calls this preposterous. Well, it is preposterous! Yet that *seems* to be what "behavioral" means. However, advocates of behavioral objectives know that such objectives serve to *further define* "understanding." Thus it may be time to suggest that an insistence upon uniform interpretation of an essentially fuzzy concept, "behavioral," may not be an issue worth the battle.

What might be gained if the adjective "behavioral" is recognized as excess baggage and is dropped? For one thing, those who use objectives could clarify their intent with adjectives more descriptive of that intent. Some objectives expressed in performance terms could be correctly identified as "cognitive" objectives. Some of these could be classed as *"conceptual"* objectives, a subset of the cognitive domain.

## Deriving Objectives

The mere use of different labels, however, certainly will not convince the critics that behaviorists are going cognitive. Conviction is not the goal of more descriptive terms, but clarity is. Those who use objectives need to clarify their own intent as much for themselves as for their critics. As will be seen, clarity depends in large measure upon the way in which objectives are derived.

Heading the list of 16 "objections" to behavioral objectives from MacDonald-Ross (1973) are the following two:

1. No consistent view exists as to the origin of objectives.
2. In the educational domain no well-defined prescriptions are available for deriving objectives (p. 41).

These problems have been with us for some time. Bobbitt (1924) advised educators to express objectives in terms of student performance. Similar, implicit concerns appeared in the early writing of the Herbartian disciples (see, for example, Wiget, 1888). Early practitioners who attempted to follow these admonitions experienced difficulty when deriving objectives. Improved analysis techniques have reduced some of the difficulties, but use of these techniques is limited. Analysis of educational goals, proposed as a process for deriving meaningful objectives (Tiemann, 1969; Mager, 1972), certainly has not gained the currency of a consistent view. Systematic attempts to identify goals by means of needs assessment, for example Kaufman (1972), share similar obscurity in educational circles.

### Task Analysis

One consistent view of the origin of some objectives does exist. Referred to as task analysis, this process for deriving objectives is relatively well-defined. But excess enthusiasm for this model has brought forth justifiable criticism (Travers, 1968) which, unfortunately, has spread to behavioral objectives in general. A consideration of task analysis reveals the reasons for the problems of acceptance among educators.

Task analysis has a long history. Its roots are found in the industrial sector (Taylor, 1911). The work of the Gilbreths in time and motion study created further interest. Gradually the techniques of task analysis began to emerge. The application of such techniques to the planning of training began to be recognized both by vocational educators (Selvidge and Fryklund, 1930) and by industrial psychologists (Viteles, 1932). Formal techniques for such use began to develop during the 1940s (Fryklund, 1942). The increased demand for training occasioned by the growth of both the military and industrial sectors during the Second World War expanded the flow of research and development funds, thereby increasing the talent pool and the level of sophistication of analysis techniques and applications.

Many types of analytical procedures exist and may be applied to derive valid objectives. Critics opposed to such applications in the educational domain often regard the resulting objectives as guilty by association. While unfortunate, this conclusion has reasonable origins. If task analysis is viewed solely as a means for locating tasks to be performed, this indeed leads to a very narrow conception of education. However, it must be remembered that task analysis is concerned with the *content* of tasks. The focus upon content is crucial. It enables a merger of analytical techniques with what is known about learning (see, for example, Gagne, 1970) and leads to prescriptive learning theory, an emphasis which is recognized as essential (Glaser, 1976). For example, two task analyses from which prescriptive objectives can be derived are presented here to illustrate the close relationship between such analysis and learning. These examples are analyses of a sequential task and a conceptual task.

**Behavior chains**. In the first type of task analysis, the sequential task used is of a familiar sort, known technically as a behavior chain. The particular chain is the task of suctioning a tracheostomy. It is performed by a nurse who uses a suction device to withdraw excessive mucus collecting in the throat of a tracheostomy (throat-incised) patient.

Although basically a cognitive task, some of the steps in suctioning a tracheostomy require *response (psychomotor) learning*. Using a smooth, coordinated twisting motion, the nurse must withdraw the suction device from a plastic retainer fitted into the tracheal incision without causing undue discomfort to the patient.

This response requires initial practice together with coaching feedback from the instructor.

As is typical of tasks found in education and training, few of the motor movements required by the chain are new to the learner. Such motor responses as dial-twisting, to start the suction, and tube washing, to tidy up after completion, are generally known. Formal instruction is not necessary. The fact that these responses are part of the existing psychomotor repertoire is evident by direct observation of their performance. No inference is required.

The second type of learning involved in all chains is *mastery of required discriminations* (Tiemann and Markle, 1973). Someone who "knows" the task has learned to respond to signals (stimuli) that occur as the task steps are performed. The suctioning task requires instruction in several of these key discriminations. One is recognizing when to suction, that is, noting when the sounds of accumulated mucus (gurgling and clicking in the throat) are "sufficient" to indicate difficulty in breathing. When the nurse trainee "knows" the difference between the sounds of "sufficient" difficulty (time to suction) and lesser difficulty (check the patient later), the nurse "discriminates the stimulus." Such cognitive ability to discriminate is inferred from observation of differential responses, which are psychomotor performances.

*Association learning* is evident when a student remembers what comes next. Each stimulus, as it occurs and is discriminated, is also the signal (the occasion) for proceeding with the next response. When "sufficient" gurgling and clicking sounds are noted, that stimulus is the occasion for the next response of assembling the needed equipment near the patient. Association learning is a matter of memory. As each stimulus occurs, the skilled performer "knows" what comes next, an association, and responds accordingly. Again, cognitive ability is inferred by observing responses.

An analysis of this type is a direct prescription for the instructional objectives required. Each step of the task poses three potential teaching points: response, discrimination, and association learning. Each of the three points of each step is judged to be either a key teaching point or a probable case of prior learning. For example, one would assume that a nurse trainee would not need to practice the smooth, coordinated movements of lifting, carrying and setting down equipment. However, discriminating when to stop assembling may be a different matter. A nurse should look at a partially assembled pile of equipment and "know" something else is required, continuing the assembly until the stimulus of a complete set of equipment is discriminated.

Complete analysis of this task yields over 20 steps. Experienced instructors judge the modeling provided by a good demonstration to be sufficient for the association learning issue. That is, nurses should remember the order of steps, requiring little prompting during their own first tries. Variability is evident when instructors judge the remaining psychomotor and discrimination learning issues. Usually six or seven components of the steps are judged to be key teaching points. An instructional objective can be developed for each of these points.

Examples of representative objectives follow. Each could be expanded with full description of conditions and standards; however, these brief statements will show the prescriptive function of analysis.

  —Recognize "sufficient" breathing difficulty (gurgling and clicking in the trachea from excess mucus) which necessitates suctioning (discrimination learning).
  —Remove the nachtube from the cannula with a twisting motion which is smooth enough (not halting, jerky or abrasive) to avoid undue patient discomfort (psychomotor learning).
  —Complete each of the steps in order without reference materials or observer prompting (association learning).

This format enables an in-depth analysis of the task *content* which, in turn, provides for clear recognition of instructional intent. The "do" aspect of psychomotor learning is distinct from the "know" aspect of cognitive performance, although observable behavior is recognized as the basis for inferring the latter capability. Plans for instruction and evaluation, differing as necessary for each type of learning, can be prescribed.

Psychomotor learning requires opportunity for practice of the new responses, perhaps with instructor coaching and confirmation. The use of simulated patients might be considered when providing such practice. Association learning also requires provision for practice and review adequate to fix the order of steps in long-term memory. Discrimination learning also requires practice but its intent is somewhat different. Based upon value judgments of task criticality, access to patients, and available resources, instructional planning might extend to audiotaped recognition practice, starting with relatively gross discriminations and progressing to the fine discriminations which are required.

The objections to behavioral objectives by their critics are best considered in the context of concrete illustrations rather than in the abstract. For example, would the specific objectives set forth for the suctioning task be considered trivial? Not by patients, our nursing educators insist! While educators may look upon memory learning as demeaning, the mere fact that some aspect of learning requires memory is a completely inappropriate basis for the judgment that it is trivial.

Turning to another concern, can the enormous number of objectives resulting from such specificity be dealt with, or even remembered by a teacher? Critics have no cause for alarm; the answer is yes. Teaching the suctioning task requires attention to only half a dozen key points and, once revealed by analysis, these are quite familiar to a qualified instructor. Such analysis, in fact, operates to clarify instructional intent and to reduce confusion and memory overload.

Analysis of instructional content requires time and effort. Is it justified? No simple prescription exists for a non-trivial answer. Essentially, the question at issue is one of level of specificity of objectives. For the tracheostomy task, a decision is possible between at least two levels, i.e., the above objectives illustrating a very specific level and a more general task level that could be indicated as follows:

   —Suction a tracheostomy when necessary. Follow standard
   procedures. Keep patient at ease with no undue anxiety or
   physical discomfort.

MacDonald-Ross (1973) noted, "The level of specificity problem has never been solved." One would hope such critics are not searching for simple prescriptions to substitute for the host of value judgments required. Representative factors to consider include the nature of the task, the performance context and logistic considerations.

For example, a senior nurse of a small hospital who plans to demonstrate the suctioning procedure to one trainee is not likely to view the analysis effort as justified, preferring instead to use the more general objective. An education director of a national hospital association preparing curriculum plans and materials for use with significant numbers of trainees probably should reach a different conclusion.

Of the many objections to more specific objectives, the notion that they are ambiguous is certainly a peculiar one. Its origin deserves consideration. Many proponents of behavioral objectives have advocated the use of action verbs in preference to verbs of state, apparently in the belief that this simplified guideline would aid others in following the suggestions set forth by Mager (1961). Such simplicity has attracted the naive and many have jumped to an erroneous conclusion concerning it. Presumably, if the right "action verb" could be found, then somehow the resulting objective would magically guide the course of instruction and evaluation.

Unfortunately, critics of behavioral objectives have accepted such arguments despite their faulty logic. For example, MacDonald-Ross (1973) cited ambiguity as an objection, basing his attack on the linguistically sound argument that "most verbs do not fit comfortably in either category." The argument, of course, is quite valid. Mager (1961) noted ambiguity to be relative, simply pointing out that some *words* (he did not use the term "verbs") were open to fewer interpretations than others.

Ambiguity exists when instructional intent is not clear. The general level objective for the suctioning task is a good example. While stated in terms of student performance, it is essentially ambiguous. It represents a mixed assortment of "know" and "do" aspects which remain to be clarified by analysis of the instructional content in terms of types of learning at issue. No amount of verb substitution or other forms of rewording and editing will "disambiguate" the key teaching points. Ambiguity arising from "know" and "do" confusion becomes less of a problem as the focus of instruction shifts to higher order cognitive skills.

**Algorithms.** The cognitive "know" aspects of sequential tasks can become increasingly complex. If so, instruction in the "do" aspects may be of less concern. For example, computing an arithmetic mean requires a step-by-step procedure but the psycho-motor responses of number-writing or calculator button-pressing are usually a matter of prior learning. Such sequences are referred to as algorithmic tasks.

Algorithms are procedural guides which confront the performer with decision points and possible branches to follow. A learner who "knows" an algorithm, having mastered the cognitive processes required by its decision points, can follow its steps and attain some goal. For example, one who "knows" the algorithm for long division, who follows its steps, and who avoids cognitive errors at the decision points will be consistently correct.

Algorithms are analyzed to determine their content, that is, to identify the cognitive skills required and the necessary order of steps. The format of such analysis is essentially the same as that for behavior chains and has been illustrated elsewhere (see, for example, Landa, 1974). Such analysis identifies key teaching points. Mastery of a particular algorithm simply requires practice. However, evaluation of student proficiency raises some complex issues.

Consider, for example, a student being taught the use of the quadratic formula to solve such expressions as $x^2 - 4x + 4 = 0$. Use of the formula is appropriate for a wide variety of such expressions, perhaps an infinite number. So instructors are not interested in student ability to solve just that expression. In fact, testing students with exactly the same expression encountered during instruction might enable them to "solve" the problem by rote, merely remembering the solution used before. Obviously, a different expression should be used to evaluate student proficiency. Problems arise with attempts to determine how representative the alternative expressions must be.

Analysts working with arithmetic algorithms have developed formula prescriptions which "define" the limits of the range of problems that may be drawn from the pool to which an algorithm applies. The prescription for a particular algorithm, once developed, enables "domain-referenced testing" (Hively *et al.*, 1968, 1974). While these domain definitions have been prepared for purposes of student testing, it may be inferred that the same prescriptions are appropriate in an instructional sense. Students to be tested with items representative of the total domain should be given the opportunity during instruction to practice with problems which are equally representative of the range.

**Complex cognitive learning.** The content of complex cognitive learning, extending beyond memory, poses challenging analysis problems as task domains increase in complexity. Some conceptual tasks, just as lower level cognitive tasks, can be essentially trivial. The process of identifying non-trivial conceptual tasks may require application of such analytical tools as concept networks or concept hierarchies to determine the structure of content, as well as attention to what is known about the acquisition of complex cognitive learning.

Earlier, a sample analysis of a chain task showed how types of learning may be considered in order to derive non-trivial objectives. Such a consideration is equally functional when deriving objectives at higher levels of learning. One useful classification scheme (Tiemann and Markle, 1973) permits the structuring of complex cognitive learning into a hierarchy of three types: concept learning, principle applying and strategy learning.

An excellent example of analysis which takes into consideration the types of complex cognitive learning is found in Thiagarajan *et al*. (1974) and is based upon curriculum development by Fink and Semmel (1971). The resulting materials and procedures provide in-service and pre-service teachers with instruction in the overall task of maintaining classroom control. Figure 1 presents one of their concept hierarchies, often a useful starting point, from which conceptual objectives can be derived.

A concept hierarchy functions as an analytical tool to represent the structure of the content, with Figure 1 identifying such structure for the various "methods" of classroom control. It identifies four types of behavior management, dividing three into particular methods. A second concept hierarchy, presented here as Figure 2, identifies a similar structure for types of student behavior, initially divided as on-task and off-task (Thiagarajan *et al.*, 1974).

The usefulness of such concept hierarchies is apparent when one considers the ways in which types of complex cognitive learning are applied. Control of a class requires the application of principles. Gagne (1970) sees principles as setting forth relationships between concepts, often in an "if . . . then" format. For example, *if* one pupil is disrupting the presentation of another with off-task noise, *then* use a signal demand to reestablish control with minimum disruption of the class.

Signal demand, one concept appearing in Figure 1, is a class of events. Its domain of instances includes such non-verbal signals as the stare, the pause, and the lift of a forefinger to one's lips as a "shh!" sign. Off-task noise is a class of student behavior quite familiar to most teachers. As illustrated above, one principle expresses a relationship between these two concepts, matching a method of control with a type of pupil behavior. In like manner, all other principles of control which are disclosed by analysis of the total management task will express a relationship between

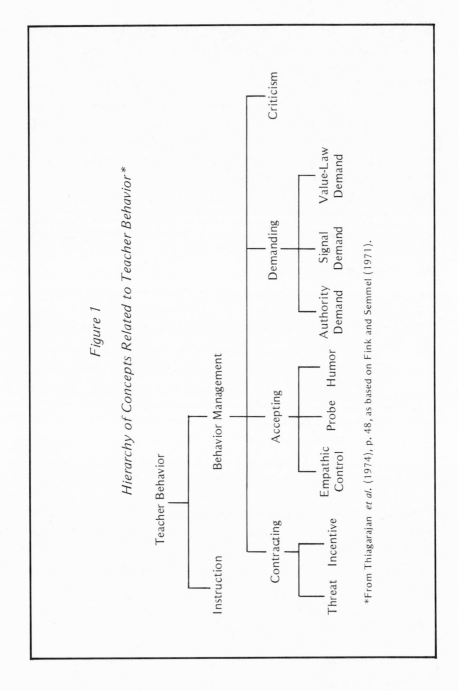

*Figure 1*

*Hierarchy of Concepts Related to Teacher Behavior**

*From Thiagarajan *et al.* (1974), p. 48, as based on Fink and Semmel (1971).

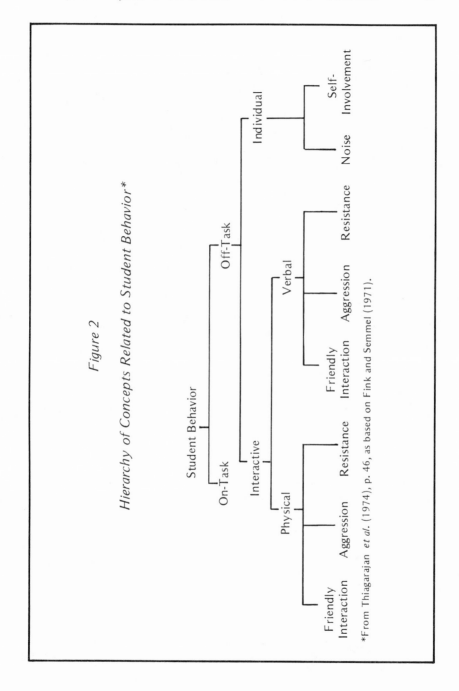

Figure 2

Hierarchy of Concepts Related to Student Behavior*

*From Thiagarajan *et al.* (1974), p. 46, as based on Fink and Semmel (1971).

concepts drawn from the two hierarchies of teacher behavior and student behavior.

Learning to apply such principles is subject to certain conditions (Gagne, 1970). In general, concepts must be understood in order for one to apply principles which subsume the concepts. In particular, a teacher must first be able to classify new instances of student behavior according to type, given a wide variety of instances representative of each type. Such performance, when observed, is the basis for inferring that the teacher "understands" the concept involved.

Next, the teacher must recall the applicable principles, thus remembering the relationship between the classified type of behavior and an appropriate method of control. Finally, the teacher must be able to employ the indicated method. While instances of performance of one method, i.e., of one concept, will vary widely across a range of "acceptable" performance, a knowledgeable observer who "understands" the permissible range of instances of the concept being employed is capable of making valid judgments about the teacher's performance.

Most experienced teachers learn to apply some of the principles which may be derived from the illustrated analysis. Faced with the daily task of maintaining control, discovery learning takes place (Bruner, 1963). Methods attempted in response to types of pupil incidents are observed to work and are repeated, or are observed not to work and are rejected. In fact, individuals acquire effective strategies which foster such discovery learning, and these strategies represent the highest level of complex cognitive learning.

However, a decision to teach teachers to apply principles of control usually is based upon the assumption that planned instruction will be more efficient and effective than discovery learning. Of course, a compromise is possible. Instruction, at first relatively structured to serve as a model of intent while revealing the application of a few principles, may shift later to a more inductive discovery mode which seems to be more challenging and appealing to most teachers.

Analysis of the classroom control process discloses "principle applying" as the appropriate goal of any instruction. In support of such ability to apply the identified principles, teachers must master the subsumed concepts. Within this framework, instructional objectives remain to be identified. Travers (1968), expressing a concern for conceptual learning, rejected the notion of behavioral objectives. He preferred to observe student performance on a sample task that was conceptual in nature and that was more open-ended than behavioral objectives would appear to permit. However, Travers saw two problems with his suggestion. First, how would the domain of a conceptual task be defined? Second, when a sample task is drawn from the domain of all possible tasks, could a teacher who observed correct student performance on that sample task then infer student ability to perform all of the tasks in the domain?

*Concept Analysis*

Analysis techniques now exist for "defining" conceptual domains, that is, for determining the range of tasks which do exist and may be sampled. The techniques also permit judgments of the representativeness of any sample drawn from the domain. These techniques are referred to as *concept analysis* (Markle and Tiemann, 1969) and may be applied to derive meaningful conceptual objectives.

> A type of objective resulting from concept analysis . . . requires the trainee to generate products or performances that fall into a specific concept category. For example, in the objectives "write a lesson plan" or "prepare an experience chart," the critical attributes of the concepts "lesson plan" and "experience chart" become the standards for the trainee products. In some other situations, we may want the trainee's performance to fall into a specific concept category (Thiagarajan *et al.*, 1974, p. 54).

As an example, Thiagarajan *et al.* (1974) present a conceptual objective derived from the critical attributes identified by analysis of one of the method concepts, "empathic control." According to their analysis, any acceptable instance of empathic control will be an act of the teacher which displays all of the following critical attributes:

—Initiated by pupil misbehavior.

—Misbehavior is not criticized.

—Expressions of understanding pupil's feelings.

—Relating pupil's behavior to his feelings (p. 54).

The resulting conceptual objective is outlined as follows:

*Performance:*   Teacher trainee shall use appropriate empathic controls.

*Range:*   ... during an actual teaching situation in a classroom.

*Conditions:*   ... without any help or prompts.

*Standards:*   1. Empathic controls should be used with at least half of the disruptive behaviors by pupils.

      2. Empathic controls should immediately follow a disruptive behavior.

      3. The teacher should express his understanding of the pupil's feelings.

      4. The teacher should relate the child's feelings to his behavior.

      5. The teacher should not criticize the child's behavior (p. 54).

The concept analysis identifies the *range* of acceptable performance. Any successful attempt must possess *all* of the identified critical attributes, which may be considered as the "defining" attributes of the concept (Klausmeier *et al.*, 1974, p. 33). If the attempt by a teacher lacks any one of the criticals, then the resulting interaction with the child is not an acceptable instance of empathic control.

A parallel issue is the rich variety of instances of good empathic control which could be exhibited by teachers. This range of variety is identified by the "irrelevant" (variable) attributes. As identified by concept analysis, Thiagarajan *et al.* (1974), lists these attributes as follows:

1. Empathic control can be initiated by any type of pupil misbehavior.
2. Statements may be made to an individual pupil or to a group of pupils.
3. Statements may or may not be accompanied by reassuring physical contact.
4. Language of the empathic statements may vary considerably (p. 48).

At this point, the concern expressed by Travers (1968) can be reassessed. He could not see how an evaluator might infer the learner's capability by extrapolating from the learner's performance on any sample task drawn from the domain. It can be seen that the performance of but one sample task is *never* sufficient evidence of conceptual understanding. What must be observed is performance on a *set* of instances, a set that is a representative sample of the rich variety identified by analysis of the domain. For instance, an evaluator would want evidence that a teacher can exert empathic control both with and without reassuring physical contact, with two students at once as well as one, and so forth. Evaluation requires several performances—the set illustrating each dimension of each of the irrelevant attributes—to assure that the teacher has mastered empathic control in its rich variation.

Mastery of concepts drawn from the student behavior hierarchy (Figure 2) is evident when the teacher observes instances of student behavior and correctly classifies such instances by type. One such concept is "physical aggression." Its critical attributes tend to be obvious, and thus only the variable attributes are illustrated here.

1. The target of physical aggression can be another person—a pupil, teacher, or someone else, or more than one person, as in the case of a single child fighting the entire class.
2. Aggression may take a wide variety of forms, such as hitting, kicking, spitting, throwing things and punching.
3. Physical aggression may or may not be accompanied by verbal aggression (insulting, abusing and swearing).

4. Physical aggression as retaliation is classified the same as an initiatory agression.
5. Physical aggression need not always take place in the classroom (Thiagarajan *et al.*, 1974, p. 45).

Adequate instruction for teachers prepared to recognize any instance of the concept requires a wide variety of examples. The range of sufficient variety is identified by the irrelevant attributes. Pairs of contrasting, "divergent" examples (Tennyson, Woolley and Merrill, 1972), which illustrate different dimensions of each of the attributes, contribute to efficient instruction. Here, for example, are two contrasting examples:

—Mary, when provoked, soundlessly kicking some other student in class.
—Mary throwing a milk carton at the cashier in the school cafeteria, apparently without provocation.

By selecting appropriate sets of such examples, which completely vary the dimensions of all of the irrelevant attributes, instruction illustrates the rich variation of the concept. Such sets of examples, representative of the domain of instances identified by analysis, constitute the essential instructional content for domain-referenced education.

Having provided such representative examples during instruction, it is appropriate to test across the same range. However, *different* examples must be reserved for testing. Conceptual understanding can be inferred only when teachers can recognize new, previously unencountered examples, that, as a set, are representative of the total domain.

Teachers must also learn to reject other kinds of pupil interaction that are close to but not quite instances of the concept, those which lack only one of the critical attributes. Concept analysis is used to locate such sets of close-in non-examples to be used in teaching and to be reserved for testing. Representative sets of previously unencountered non-examples also must be reserved for testing in order to measure other than memory learning.

Conceptual instruction and evaluation, accomplished with sets of examples and non-examples representative of the range of a concept, as disclosed by its analysis, are critical components of domain-referenced education.

Three further concerns with respect to behavioral objectives, each quite significant, may be examined in reference to the notion of conceptual objectives. One criticism arises from apparent description of the product with little attention to the process of learning. One form of such criticism (e.g., Waks, 1969) is all too evident. Algebra instructors complain that students get right answers but do not understand a process. Often, the process is step-by-step, an algorithm. Such algorithms, when analyzed to identify cognitive learning required at their decision points, are shown to require conceptual ability, e.g., mastery of such concepts as "associativity" or "distributivity." Instruction directed primarily to the association learning aspects, i.e., recalling an order of steps, may overlook the conceptual requirements of algorithms. Exposed to such instruction, students follow the steps, essentially by rote, and fail to "understand." Such instruction deserves the criticism typical of training, i.e., learning the how but not the why. Domain-referenced education, with emphasis upon analysis to identify both the conceptual aspects of such processes and their domains, requires the derivation of conceptual objectives which prescribe appropriate instructional events.

A closely-related concern regarding behavioral objectives is their possible inability to deal with the process of appreciation. Eisner (1969) would prefer objectives that engage students in the interpretation of meaning of an artistic work or event. He stated:

> In this context the mode of evaluation is similar to aesthetic criticism; that is, the critic appraises a product, examines its qualities and import . . . . The critic's subject matter is the work done—he does not prescribe a blueprint of its construction (p. 16).

Again, the relevant student performance should not result in a product, a blueprint. As Eisner suggests, aesthetic criticism is the *process* of concern, the relevant activity of appreciation. It is an evaluative, judgmental process. Incorporating value judgments, the activity is of concern to the educational philosopher and its process is analyzed as follows:

> First, there must be an object, event, or something to consider; second, there must be a set of criteria which incorporate the preferences of the individual or group involved in the considera- tion; third, there are facts about whatever is being evaluated which indicate that the criteria are applicable to it; and finally, a judgment is rendered and a rating is made of whatever it is that is being evaluated (Broudy, Smith and Burnett, 1964, p. 147).

The important function of criteria when concerned with process is reflected in the earlier illustration of analysis of classroom control concepts. When a teacher observes a new instance of student behavior and correctly classifies it as "physical aggres- sion," one can infer some conceptual mastery by that teacher. A subtle difference exists in the case of a second concept, "empathic control." While the performance of the student resulted in an instance of "physical aggression," it is the performance of the *teacher* which must result in an instance of "empathic control."

As noted before, an observer in the role of evaluator might class a teacher's performance as an acceptable instance of the concept "empathic control." If the observer can classify a sufficient range of performances as such, then one may infer mastery of the concept by the observer functioning in the role of evaluator. Similarly, the observer may *appreciate* the performance of the teacher in terms of the rich variety of empathic control evident in the skilled performance. In this case, the attributes of the concept would constitute the appraisal criteria. The degree of appreciation would be a function of the number of concepts mastered by the observer. Thus, appreciation increases as the competent teacher is observed to perform more "methods" of control, each in a rich variety. But it is the observer who, on the basis of conceptual understanding, is appreciating.

Smith (1969) poses the question, "What does appreciation mean in terms of other concepts?" He believes behavioral objectives are just "nonsense" if their use does not permit educators to deal with that question, supporting the contention that conceptual understanding is basic to appreciation.

The function of conceptual objectives also extends to issues of values and norms. The remarks of Broudy, Smith and Burnett cited earlier occurred in relation to their recommendations directed to restoring democracy and excellence in the curriculum, specifically in their chapter titled "Content as Valuative Concepts and Norms." A reasoned argument is advanced for considering the judgment process employed in respect to individual values and social norms to be conceptual and the appropriate concern of education.

> At a time when the valuative principles of the social system are themselves in conflict, it becomes necessary to reconstruct them, to reshape them to meet new conditions. This requires of the citizen a fairly high level of logical ability to handle concepts and principles charged with strongly held preferences (Broudy, Smith and Burnett, 1964, p. 153).

An education responsive to these requirements will be domain-referenced, with analysis used to identify and clarify the key concepts and principles that influence student attitudes, appreciations and value systems. These become the content of conceptual objectives, extending to normative and valuative concerns.

## Operational Approaches Versus Conceptual Approaches

Another criticism of behavioral objectives, perhaps the most significant, derives from the weakness of the logic of operationalism and the fact that such logic often is used to render objectives in behavioral format (Smith, 1972; MacDonald-Ross, 1973). Operationalism employs "if and only if" statements. One example provided by Zais (1976) defines strength operationally: "If *200 pushups* plus *lifts 150-pound barbell*, then *and only then* strength" (p. 314). Zais adds:

> As a definition of strength for, say, research purposes, such a statement might, because of its restrictedness and precision, be quite useful.... But are curriculum workers willing thus to

> restrict the meaning of their objectives for learners? To do so is to
> fall into the delusion that the two behaviors *are* strength, and that
> the construct is being directly measured (p. 314).

Operationalism can be seen as a process of defining abstract
constructs or concepts in terms of a limited number of instances
drawn from their domains. "Signal demand," for example, might
be defined by two of its instances such that it occurs if and only if
a teacher stares at a student and emits a "shh" sound. The task of
mastering the "concept" thus defined, when its domain of
instances normally spans a rich variety, is reduced to rote memory.
The teacher needs remember one and only one performance, one
limited type of instance.

In contrast, analysis of concepts such as "signal demand"
identifies the attributes which, then, define the domain. Conceptual instruction requires a variety of representative specimens.
Conceptual understanding is assessed with an equivalent variety of
previously unencountered specimens. Conceptual objectives guiding such instruction result from an analysis procedure which
specifically avoids the weakness inherent in the logic of operationalism. Attributes, rather than instances, define the concept.

An operational mode of teaching has drawbacks of a parallel
type. Broudy, Smith and Burnett (1964) provide an hypothetical
illustration in teaching the concept "democracy," where operational teaching places a student in situations requiring democratic
behavior:

> He learns to behave democratically under these circumstances,
> and perhaps to like this way of doing things. But what he fails to
> acquire is a clear verbalization of the concept of democracy . . . .
> He cannot analyze the concept into its elements and make them
> explicitly clear, nor is he able to meet the cogent arguments of
> those who hold a contrary view (p. 137).

Advocates of conceptual teaching have suggested that complete
student mastery of defined concepts is evident only when students
can respond correctly to instances of the concept, in this case
"democracy," as well as verbalize correctly the attributes of the
concept (see, for example, Klausmeier *et al.*, 1974). Others have

advocated conceptual teaching in preference to memory learning because the latter typically results only in an ability to spout a serial memory definition, even though such a verbalization might include the more important attributes of the concept.

A domain-referenced approach to education, while definitely concerned with conceptual understanding, need not rule out a concern for verbal information. In fact, the "domain" of such memory tasks can be viewed simply as unity. Analysis techniques required of a domain-referenced approach serve to identify and clarify such content issues and to prescribe appropriate instructional and evaluation procedures.

### The Outlook for Domain-Referenced Education

While central to the process of domain-referenced education, the appropriate analysis techniques require significant time both to master and to apply. The current structure of our educational system seldom provides teachers with sufficient time to engage in the amount of analysis required. System-wide benefits might result if such analysis could provide a basis for the design and development of published instructional materials. If so, educational personnel would require training to select and to employ domain-referenced materials. Such training would require conceptual objectives. Appreciation of the rationale of domain-referenced education would be essential. However, the required quality of materials, due to analysis supported financially by publishers, could not be maintained unless school personnel understood the origin of such quality and insisted that the system pay for it.

An initial move toward domain-referenced education might well reveal some inadequacies, perhaps some overemphasis upon lower level cognitive objectives. As suggested by Popham (1976), the emphasis of domain-referenced testing could be expected to shift to "larger," more significant concepts. The shift could be expected to continue, gradually extending to deliberate instruction in general problem-solving skills, as represented in the work of Larkin and Reif (1976). Eventually, deliberate instruction in strategies of learning might be common-place. Resnick and her colleagues (e.g., Resnick, Siegel and Kresh, 1971; Resnick, Wang and Kaplan, 1973) are investigating ways to instruct children so that children develop their own information-processing skills, often more efficient and effective than the models used during their instruction. Sophisticated analytical techniques are required by such efforts. The techniques themselves must be the subject of further improvement in support of domain-referenced education.

## Summary

The attributes of the concept of domain-referenced education have been identified. Critical attributes include appropriate analysis of domains, instruction with content representative of such domains, and domain-referenced evaluation matched to the type of learning. In particular, concept learning requires evidence that students can deal with situations new to them. The variable attributes include goals (which may be cognitive, affective, or valuative) and levels of learning (which may vary from simple memory to the most complex cognitive skills). The probable focus on domain-referenced education will be high level complex cognitive skills. This focus will require continued efforts to develop and improve the analytical techniques required for deriving meaningful conceptual objectives.

## References

Bobbitt, F. *How to Make a Curriculum*. Boston: Houghton Mifflin, 1924.

Broudy, H.S., B.O. Smith and J.R. Burnett. *Democracy and Excellence in American Secondary Education*. Chicago: Rand McNally, 1964.

Bruner, J.S. *The Process of Education*. Cambridge, Mass.: Harvard University Press, 1963.

Eisner, E.W. Instructional and Expressive Educational Objectives: Their Formulation and Use in Curriculum, in *Instructional Objectives*, AERA Monograph Series on Curriculum Evaluation No. 3, Ed. R.E. Stake. Chicago: Rand McNally, 1969.

Fink, A.H. and M.I. Semmel. *Indiana Behavior Management System-II.* Bloomington, Ind.: Center for Innovation in Teaching the Handicapped, Indiana Univ., 1971.

Fryklund, V.C. *Trade and Job Analysis.* Milwaukee: Bruce, 1942.

Gagne, R.M. *The Conditions of Learning,* 2nd Ed. New York: Holt, Rinehart and Winston, 1970.

Glaser, R. Components of a Psychology of Instruction: Toward a Science of Design. *Review of Educational Research,* Winter 1976, *46,* 1-24.

Hively, W., H. Patterson and S. Page. A Universe Defined System of Arithmetic Tests. *Journal of Educational Measurement,* Winter 1968, *5,* 275-290.

Hively, W. *et al. Domain-Referenced Testing.* Englewood Cliffs, N.J.: Educational Technology Publications, 1974.

Kaufman, R.A. *Educational Systems Planning.* Englewood Cliffs, N.J.: Prentice-Hall, 1972.

Klausmeier, H.J., E.S. Ghatala and C.A. Frayer. *Conceptual Learning and Development: A Cognitive View.* New York: Academic Press, 1974.

Landa, L.N. *Algorithmization in Learning and Instruction.* Englewood Cliffs, N.J.: Educational Technology Publications, 1974.

Larkin, J.H. and F. Reif. Analysis and Teaching of a General Skill for Studying Scientific Text. *Journal of Educational Psychology,* August 1976, *68,* 431-440.

MacDonald-Ross, M. Behavioral Objectives: A Critical Review. *Instructional Science,* May 1973, *2,* 1-52.

MacMillan, C.J.B. and J.E. McClellan. Can and Should Means-End Reasoning Be Used in Teaching? in *Concepts of Teaching: Philosophical Essays,* Ed. MacMillan and Nelson. Chicago: Rand McNally, 1968, 375-406.

Mager, R.F. *Preparing Objectives for Programmed Instruction.* San Francisco: Fearon, 1961.

Mager, R.F. *Preparing Instructional Objectives.* Palo Alto: Fearon, 1962.

Mager, R.F. *Goals Analysis.* Belmont, Cal.: Fearon, 1972.

Markle, S.M. and P.W. Tiemann. *Really Understanding Concepts: or, in Frumious Pursuit of the Jabberwock.* Champaign, Ill.: Stipes, 1969.

Popham, W.J. Expanding the Technical Base of Criterion-Referenced Test Development. Presentation to the AERA annual meeting, San Francisco, April, 1976.

Resnick, L.B., A.W. Siegel and E. Kresh. Transfer and Sequence in Learning Double Classification Skills. *Journal of Experimental Child Psychology,* February 1971, *11,* 139-149.

Resnick, L.B., M.C. Wang and J. Kaplan. Task Analysis in Curriculum Design: A Hierarchically Sequenced Introductory Mathematics Curriculum. *Journal of Applied Behavior Analysis,* Winter 1973, *6,* 679-710.

Selvidge, R.W. and V.C. Fryklund. *Principles of Trade and Industrial Teaching.* Peoria, Ill.: Manual Arts Press, 1930.

Smith, P.G. On the Logic of Behavioral Objectives. *Phi Delta Kappan*, March 1972, *53*, 429-431.

Taylor, F.W. *Shop Management*. New York: Harper, 1911.

Tennyson, R.D., F.R. Woolley and M.D. Merrill. Exemplar and Nonexemplar Variables Which Produce Correct Classification Behavior and Specified Classification Errors. *Journal of Educational Psychology*, April 1972, *63*, 144-152.

Thiagarajan, S., D.S. Semmel and M.I. Semmel. *Instructional Development for Training Teachers of Exceptional Children: A Sourcebook*. Blooming-ton, Ind.: Center for Innovation in Teaching the Handicapped (LTI U. Minn., CITH Ind. U., CEC), 1974.

Tiemann, P.W. Analysis and the Derivation of Valid Objectives. *NSPI Journal*, July 1969, *8*, 16-18.

Tiemann, P.W. and S.M. Markle. Remodeling a Model: An Elaborated Hierarchy of Types of Learning. *Educational Psychologist*, Fall 1973, *10*, 147-158.

Travers, R.M.W. Models of Education and Their Implications for the Conduct of Evaluation Studies. Presentation to the AERA annual meeting. Chicago: February, 1968.

Viteles, M.S. *Industrial Psychology*. New York: W.W. Norton, 1932.

Waks, L.J. Philosophy, Education and the Doomsday Threat. *Review of Educational Research*, December 1969, *39*, 607-621.

Wiget, T. *Die Formalen Stufen des Unterrichts, eine Einfuhrung in die Schriften Zillers*. 3rd Ed. Chur: Verlag von Rich, 1888.

Zais, R.S. *Curriculum Principles and Foundations*. New York: Thomas Y. Crowell, 1976.

# 4.
# Education, Training and Behavioral Objectives

### George L. Geis

Before turning to the primary focus of this chapter—kinds, examples and uses of behavioral objectives—it is useful to look briefly at the words "educational technology," under which behavioral objectives have often been subsumed or categorized. The "technology" aspect of educational technology—its sources and its applications—was not really developed in the world of education. It sprang, for the most part, from those involved in training. Even the star performers in this technology who are associated with education (for example, Susan Markle, Robert Glaser, Richard Anderson) have often directed their efforts at areas which lie in the overlap of training and education. Several of these wiser heads have opted for a phrase like "instructional technology" which does not carry with it, or rather pull after it, associations surrounding the word "education."

Other problems attach to the word "technology"—namely that it usually refers to the application of scientific principles which have been precisely worked out, stated and tested under conditions which most scientists would agree were scientific. However, much of *educational* technology is lore, highly sophisticated and devised by people with insight and creativity, but lore, nevertheless. That concern ought to be prominent in a comprehensive discussion of behavioral objectives, because only a small amount of research has been conducted in this area and most of it does not clearly demonstrate the purported benefits.

## Discriminating Between Training
## and Education

These introductory observations suggest the two main themes of this chapter, as follows:

1. That the transference of a technology of instruction to the world of traditional education should not be made without consideration of the differences between training and education, *and* cannot be made quickly and easily.

2. That some of the uneasiness about "objectives," even after a decade or more of proselytizing and promotion, is due to basic differences between training and traditional education in the approach to subject matter—to the "stuff" with which the teacher deals.

One traditional way of discriminating between training and education is to define training as teaching toward goals which can be explicitly pre-defined. It is implied that the terminal behaviors of the training episode can be described in terms of the physical responses to be emitted by the trainee. Education, on the other hand, often is used to refer, at least in the narrower sense, to situations in which the terminal behavior *itself* cannot be defined. While this distinction may be challenged, it is a useful one to make whether or not the reader agrees to label the two categories as "training" and "education."*

Sometimes final behaviors can be precisely defined because they are emitted by experts. That means that the behavior exists; it is observable; the task is repeatedly executed by people "on the job." Developing behavioral objectives in such cases involves accurate recording and sophisticated analysis of an existing performance.

In some areas of training, however, the task must be designed (e.g., the operator's job when given a new machine) rather than

---

*Some people have stressed a distinction between *instruction* and *education*. This discrimination overlaps the one I am trying to make, but it is not exactly isomorphic with mine.

observed. In such cases, the *product* or *output* of the task is often definable; it can be observed and its quality can be described. Various performances can be tried out and the "correctness" of the performance can be defined in terms of the "goodness" of the product.

The world of education is not a world of tasks and work. (It is important to note that the word "education" will be used in the ensuing pages to refer, for the most part, to secondary and post-secondary education. Most elements in the primary school curriculum, as well as many of those in post-secondary education, can best be classified as "training," as defined above.) Traditionally, the world of education is a world of *content*. Something vaguely called *knowledge* is at the core of all that the educator does. And the analyses that are made tend to be in terms of *content* analysis (e.g., Bloom, 1956, and Krathwohl *et al.*, 1964) rather than in terms of *task* analysis. (Knowledge may include "talking about" behavior, and the behaviorists may claim that talk itself is behavior. But, for practical purposes, such distinctions amount to quibbling.) In most situations, when the educator thinks of what he is going to teach, he does not think of a performance or task but rather of a subject matter. Indeed, the old saw that "those who can do and those who can't teach" may be relevant at this point. Knowledge is not, at least in the traditional meaning of the word, behavior.*

I am well aware of the attacks on behavioral objectives emanating from those who misunderstand, those who are lazy, and those who for too long have been successfully manufacturing and selling "fuzzies." Most of those attacks, when looked at carefully,

---

*For purposes of this discussion, academic goals are examined that have at least some analogy to training goals. Of course, some people have assigned to schools sets of goals far different from, and far beyond, these. For example, to some the school is a surrogate family and to others it is primarily a means of instilling values and/or conformity to the society in which it operates. These kinds of purposes or "goals" lend themselves even less to the usual language and procedures of stating behavioral objectives.

seem to be beside the point. However, when viewed superficially, many of them represent part of a strong and large-scale resistance to *systematic instruction* and to the development of a technology of education.

A setback—a confusing pause in the development of that technology—occurs when we engage in disputation. Such setbacks are especially pronounced when the debaters ignore some basic differences between education and training as well as some underlying semantic difficulties. I, for one, do not want to spend time "defending" behavioral objectives. If behavioral objectives are useful in producing better instruction in a particular milieu, given a particular population of instructors—fine! If not—and this is important—a rigid insistance upon the use of behavioral objectives instead of the offering of an acceptable and sound alternative is non-productive. Furthermore, in the heat of argument, the concept of a systematic approach to education may be damaged. As a consequence, often the baby does get tossed out with the bath water (e.g., Szilak, 1976).

A case is being made by a number of us who are engaged in translating the "technology of instruction" into a "technology of education" that what is *really* meant by "knowledge" can be stated *in terms of* behavior. Furthermore, we contend that the outcomes of education can be made observable, describable and measurable. The point is that this is not an easy translation to make. A simple-minded application of a technology that is based upon observable and analyzable tasks to the teaching of "academic" content is likely to run into trouble. And that has happened. Quite aside from the resistance being offered on the grounds of emotion, more telling points have been made.

For example, insistence upon the behavioral specification of goals has been said to lead to the generation of trivial and superficial objectives. And though we pooh-poohed that prophecy, it has proved true in many instances. Partly because educators are unused to thinking in the way that trainers are, trivial objectives abound while the larger goals of education remain amorphous, mysterious and indescribable. I would maintain that observable terminal behaviors can be stated for courses in language appreciation, critical thinking or problem-solving, and even more easily for courses in medical diagnosis, historical research or prose composition. But I have come to appreciate the *difficulty* of doing so, and I recoil at most of the responses I have seen to being forced to do so.

Complicating the task of analysis is the fact that the teacher usually does not have the terminal performers readily available for study. The trainer, on the other hand, can easily go into the field and observe a model performer. Except for some examples from professional schools, teachers do not study the jobs for which their pupils are preparing. *Indeed*, they often argue that there is no "job"—that they are not preparing them for a task at all!

School teachers in particular not only do not have access to many of the final behaviors which their curriculum implies, but they have not traditionally been placed in the position of deciding upon major terminal goals. The trivializing of objective-stating may be as much a function of that as of other factors.

The difference between training and education may be clarified further by looking at evaluation materials. Under the best conditions the final act of a training episode involves the execution of the task-relevant behavior—that is, the "test." To take a simple-minded example, if the objective is to teach swimming, the best test, of course, would be to observe the student swimming at the conclusion of instruction. Where the emission of the actual performance would be dangerous or expensive, a simulation may be evoked. In education, the actual "terminal behavior" is called for much less frequently. Usually a *sample* rather than a complete performance is called for, and often it is a *correlated sample*. Let us look at these terms.

If our objective were to teach someone to swim five hundred yards within a certain period of time, the best test would be to observe whether or not he could swim the distance in that period of time. For various reasons (e.g., time constraints) we might ask

him to swim only one hundred yards. Then we would *predict*, if
he could swim the one hundred yards in a certain time period
(perhaps breathing at a certain rate, etc.), that he could continue
on for another four hundred yards. Such a test might be labelled
"partial performance." It is a sample of the whole performance,
but a particular kind of sample. It is actually a piece of the
terminal behavior. A slightly different kind of sample might
involve a demonstration of kicks and strokes in the water. These
would be components of the final performance but not really a
segment of it. (Once we start sampling, we are assuming that some
part of the whole predicts the whole. On the basis of previous data
we should be able to assert that anyone who can exhibit those
components in that style can indeed swim for five hundred yards.)
Even more "iffy" would be a test in which the student was asked
to name various strokes or describe in words the sequence of
coordinations involved in swimming. Clearly this is not a segment
or a component of the final performance. In such a case we *must*
have evidence of correlation (as well as, incidentally, test security).

### Objectives and Evaluation

It may occur to the reader at this point that most "behavioral
objectives," including those that meet the technical requirements
prescribed by experts, tend to be partial terminal performances,
samples of components or correlated samples. Thus: "Given a
pencil and paper, the child upon hearing the words 'circle' and
'triangle' will draw first a circle and then a triangle." Or: "Given a
black and white drawing of a blood cell, the student will be able to
label the major parts of the cell correctly by writing their names
next to the arrows which point to the appropriate parts." These
behavioral objectives contain the generally agreed-upon components (e.g., an observable *response*, under specified *conditions*, as
defined by explicit or implicit *criteria*), but these objectives are,
nevertheless, clearly of a different sort than "observing the final
swimming performance of the swimming student." In fact, one
might question whether such objectives are really test items rather

than objectives at all. Simplistic answers like "It doesn't matter which they are," or "They are both the same," can be applied legitimately only when the intended test is a *complete* perfor- mance. Otherwise, there *is* a difference between the objective and its "test," "indicator," "symptom" or whatever.

The uneasiness that teachers have expressed upon producing objectives such as the ones just stated is well-founded. At best these are sub-objectives or intermediate objectives. At worst they are the illegitimate children of unknown objectives and poorly worked out test items.

Since one of the major benefits of producing good behavioral objectives is that one can *then* produce better evaluation material, I would suggest that the professor or teacher be encouraged to examine, usually in cooperation with an expert in instructional design, the evaluation materials that he or she has at hand. In such situations it can be pointed out, for example, that the evaluation materials are operationalizations of the goals or meaning of the course to the students. Such evaluation materials also describe the meaning of the course to those who are accepting the grade of the student as an indication of competence. In fact, they are the evidences from which goals may be induced.

When asking for the test materials, the consultant may well expect that his client will demure. (A catalog of handy phrases might be offered by the consultant to the client in order to save time. These include such comments as, "I don't think this exam tests what I really teach." Or, "This exam is just a test of memory. You can't test the more important things in the course." And so forth.) But with enough perseverance and good will, current test materials can be used to generate better evaluation designs. In many cases involving training, for example, the test may involve the exhibition of a complete, real-world performance or it may involve a simulation. To the degree that the test material under development moves away from real-world performance, time must be invested in verifying that the correlated sample is a valid measure. For instance, does the fact that I know that the *tu* form in French is to be used with pets, domestics and mistresses really indicate anything about my proficiency in using the language? If I can name the Presidents of the United States, do I have a sense of history and will I be a better citizen? These examples *seem* almost absurd, yet perhaps there *is* a correlation between such test responses and more global kinds of behaviors. On the other hand, some test items seem to have a great deal of "face validity." In any case, it is presumptuous and dangerous to eliminate or accept any proposed test items on an *a priori* basis. Correlation ought to be *empirically* determined.

*There* is the catch! It is at the point of attempting to set up the correlational study that the teacher or professor must move from discussing content to discussing performance. On what basis does he hypothesize that naming the Presidents is correlated with a sense of history, or, that stating the rule for the use of *tu* rather than *vous* is prerequisite to fluent and appropriate social or business conversations in French?

In many cases the correlations that are sought may be internal for the next stage of instruction. That is to say, they may indicate the extent to which a student has the prerequisites for the next stage of instruction. There may be objections to this strategy of demonstrating that a high score on Test A indicates that a student is ready for Instructional Episode B. The whole effort may result in a curriculum that shows high internal consistency but has no relationship to the "real-world." But such internal consistency and the previous demonstration of the usefulness (within the curriculum) of each item being taught and tested is not to be scoffed at. Indeed, the first step to good pedagogy, as contrasted to good training, may be to provide a well-working system of instruction. Then the validity of the goals can be examined by those who are both inside and outside the given educational system.

Some people might criticize the procedure just suggested as being "an awfully big job!" In fact, it is likely to be not only big but challenging. The exercise in correlation, for example, may provide the basis for new and in-depth questioning of certification requirements. It could reactivate in a new context (and with new ground rules) dormant debates on defining "good" historians, scholars, scientists, citizens and, even, societies. Let us not forget that throughout the history of man's intellectual activities—long predating time and motion studies and cost-benefit analyses—great thinkers have wrestled with the kinds of questions to which the exercise in correlation may well lead in some disciplines. It remains to be seen whether or not members of those disciplines are ready to exchange cheap shots at behavioral objectives for the intense, difficult and self-revealing discussions this procedure will produce.

The suggestion in this chapter is that the time and labor being spent on extracting (and the use of the term from dentistry seems appropriate) behavioral objectives from teachers might as well be spent in devising good methods of evaluation. Conversely, full-time instructional designers (even when they are approaching areas that traditionally have been the exclusive domain of education) may well deal more efficiently with instruction and learning problems by first generating behavioral objectives and then working at evaluation systems.

## Conclusions

The activity centered around behavioral objectives over the past decade has been a dynamic force in education as well as in training. Implicit in this chapter are several positive points:

1. The field of education can learn much from the technology being developed outside of it.

2. The field of education ought to pursue the development of a technology within itself.

3. The translation of a technology of instruction derived from areas that are outside of traditional education requires sophisticated handling.

4. The field of education, and especially educational psychology, can contribute to the next decade of instructional technology in an area in which educational psychologists have much experience and many expert practitioners—the area of evaluation.

5. Devising good instruments to evaluate learning may produce for education benefits that are equivalent to those now claimed by proponents of behavioral objectives.

6. The need for well-stated objectives in education remains. The problem is how and when to get them. The development of sophisticated behavioral objectives requires a great deal of previous training and insight. We must also be willing to spend time developing nearly equal skills in the user.

The behavioral objectives "movement" has had a dramatic and beneficial impact upon education. A dynamic technology must utilize observations of and reflections upon its past performances in constructing an agenda for the future.

## References

Bloom, B.S. (Ed.) *Taxonomy of Educational Objectives: Handbook I, Cognitive Domain.* New York: David McKay Company, Inc., 1956.

Krathwohl, D.R. *et al. Taxonomy of Educational Objectives: Handbook II, Affective Domain.* New York: David McKay Company, Inc., 1964.

Szilak, D. Strings: A Critique of Systematic Education. *Harvard Educational Review,* February 1976, *46,* 54-75.

# 5.
# Behavioral Objectives:
# The History and the Promise

H.H. McAshan

The long-range promise of behavioral objectives is to increase student learning by improving the quality of instruction in schools. Theoretically, this should occur as a direct consequence of improved teacher education programs in the nation's colleges and universities and as a result of improved inservice programs for practicing teachers.

To place the behavioral objectives movement into proper perspective, one should recognize that it must take its place alongside many previous movements such as team teaching, homogeneous grouping, lengthened time for instruction, modular scheduling, differentiated staffing, and new media, and a host of others. The behavioral objectives movement is subject to the same enthusiasm, political motivation, economic frustration and other forces as were all the other movements. None of these previous movements was able to transform instruction or the profession in any significant manner resembling a panacea. Each did contribute something to the learning situation, but the most significant gains were probably situation-specific and not easy to diffuse into new populations.

The behavioral objectives movement does appear to have more to offer than previous thrusts because there appears to be something in it for everyone. Persons interested in goal-setting or competency identification, in analysis and development of teaching strategies, and in program evaluation of all types can find ample opportunity to pursue their interests. Administrators concerned with program accountability can produce more overtly observable data than under the traditional experience-based approach. Researchers find new opportunities to utilize their expertise. Students become more aware of what they are expected to learn and how success will be determined. It becomes easier to communicate instructional program goals to parents.

Behavioral objectives, properly conceptualized and used, also have the potential to revolutionize teacher education. But, if the movement is going to contribute significantly, attention must be given to several continuing concerns that are rather basic to the behavioral approach. These concerns include the following:

1. Defining "learning" outcomes, defining "behavioral" outcomes, and distinguishing between the two.
2. Reaching a consensus about what is a "worthwhile" behavioral objective.
3. Coping with economic and political factors.
4. Providing coordination for the behavioral objectives movement.
5. Assessing competency based education (CBE) programs.

The purpose of this chapter will be to focus attention on these five concerns in an effort to stimulate additional thought toward their eventual resolution. No attempt will be made to rank the items or to estimate their individual weight with regard to the ultimate success of the behavioral objectives or competency based education movements. Each will be discussed in the following sections.

### "Learning" Outcomes: Goals, Competencies or Learning Intents

Learning theory indicates that learning begins when stimuli (either internal or external) and their reinforcement cause an organism to react. Learning occurs through this process, and the more complex cognitive, psychomotor and affective motivational systems develop. Thus, all learning can be said to begin when the learner is sensitized to the existence of stimuli. These stimuli may be thought of as occurring as the result of teaching strategies (or enabling activities) that are part of the instructional delivery system in CBE programs.

For the purposes of our present discussion, we will consider all learning as occurring according to a set process or format consisting of two phases, the receiving phase and the internalization phase. The receiving phase consists of four stages—the proprioceptual, preceptual, perceptual and conceptual. In the propricoceptual stage, a stimulus is picked up by one or more of the learner's primary sensory receptors. This usually involves seeing, hearing or feeling. These sensory cell receptors transmit stimuli to the central nervous system, referred to as the preceptual stage, which interprets the stimuli and gives further instructions.

From the preceptual stage the stimuli are passed on to the perceptual stage, where a mental image of the stimulus is formed and general awareness takes place. Following this awareness, the stimuli input is passed on to the conceptual stage, which results in thought formulation concerning the stimuli variables. At this point we might infer that the receiving phase is completed. The proprioceptual and preceptual stages of the receiving phases represent raw input, whereas learning actually begins to take place during the perceptual and conceptual stages of the receiving phase.

The second learning phase, the internalization phase, can be considered as the primary focus of the learning process. This is where the desired learning outcomes occur and are stored. This phase is characterized by the changes that take place within the learner and which become part of the learner. These changes represent the learner's cognitive, affective and psychomotor development or, in other words, the capabilities that the learner has acquired with reference to understandings, feelings or movement activities.

These capabilities or acquired attributes can represent many levels of learning that have occurred and are based upon the amount of internalization of feelings, understanding or movement capability that has taken place. Perhaps the best way to interpret this internalization of learning is through the taxonomies by Bloom (1956), Krathwohl *et al.* (1964) and Harrow (1972). Each of these taxonomies portrays several hierarchical levels of capabilities that can be acquired by learners through the learning process.

Figure 1 depicts the relationships among learning and the three behavioral taxonomies. It can be assumed that the outcomes of learning should result in the acquisition of capabilities which can be placed into Levels 2.00-5.00 of the affective taxonomy, 1.00-6.00 of the cognitive taxonomy and 2.00-6.00 of the psychomotor taxonomy.

It should be noted that the learning outcomes are the ends for which all enabling instructional activities are performed. Since the learning outcomes are ends, they may be viewed as having the only intrinsic value to be found in the instructional program. *These learning outcomes are the prime purposes of education.* All other components of the instructional program, such as the enabling strategies and evaluation processes, are merely *means* for producing learning outcomes or for *evaluating* successful achievement of learning outcomes.

Gagne (1974) states it this way: "What is learned is something new that remains a part of the learner. Some would call these abilities, but I prefer to speak of them as capabilities . . . . It is these capabilities that constitute the outcomes of learning" (p. 3). Gronlund (1974) supports this concept through his emphasis on *understanding* as being the objective of learning, rather than on *behavioral outcomes* which are the responses made after understanding occurs. He states that behavioral outcomes "are simply samples of the types of performance that represent understanding" (pp. 4-6). One must recognize that the learning is never purely affective, or cognitive, or psychomotor, but that the student may develop in all three areas simultaneously. The educator must choose, however, which of these three areas is of primary concern at any particular time when formulating the competencies and/or objectives to be achieved.

*Figure 1*

*Relationships Among Learning and the Behavioral Taxonomies*

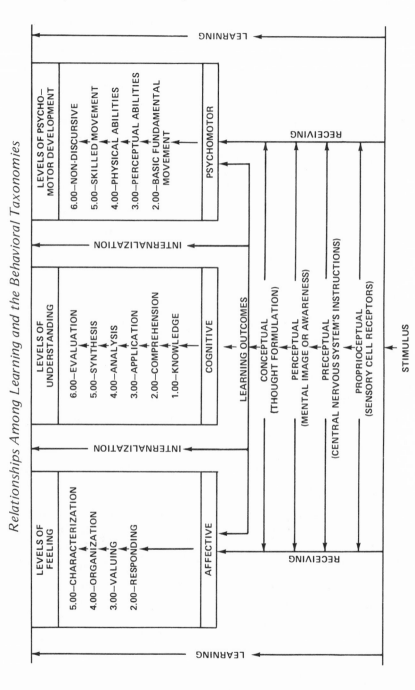

Regardless of a person's acceptance or non-acceptance of the hierarchical nature of the taxonomies, it appears safe to say that the learning outcomes defined as the abilities or capabilities that become part of the learner should constitute the competencies which a learner should achieve. Furthermore, most educators will agree that competencies can be placed into one or more of the three domains. Thus, learning outcomes should represent the attainment of specific learning intents or competencies, and these should become the goals of instruction.

The key to writing good competency statements is to determine first the level of learning outcome that is desired for a specific skill or content unit and then to state it in terms of a specific goal to be achieved. The following two sample goal statements from a unit in PERT (Program Evaluation and Review Technique) can serve as examples for the identification of specific competencies to be achieved:

1. EDA 605 students will acquire knowledge of selected PERT terms and symbols.
2. EDA 605 students will develop the ability to apply PERT techniques in the construction of a functional control network.

Both of these goal statements identify "EDA 605 students" as being accountable for achieving the competency. The terms "will acquire" and "will develop" give the goal statements a future time orientation. In other words, they indicate that the desired learning outcome is expected to occur in the future and is not something that students can be expected to demonstrate immediately.

"Knowledge" in the first goal statement, and "the ability to apply" in the second goal statement, reveal that the amounts of internalization should be at the knowledge and application levels respectively, according to the cognitive taxonomy. "PERT terms and symbols" and "PERT techniques in the construction of a functional control network" identify the specific content to be learned.

As soon as a teacher has identified all of the learning outcomes or competencies that are appropriate for a particular unit of study and has stated the competencies in terms of specific goals, he or she is ready to begin thinking about behavioral outcomes.

### "Behavioral" Outcomes:
### Assessment Techniques

Behavioral outcomes represent the responses a learner can make through use of the abilities or capabilities that have been acquired during the learning process. They may best be thought of as assessment techniques that can be utilized to evaluate whether or not the learner has achieved the desired learning outcomes or competencies that have been prescribed for him.

The difference between a learning outcome and a behavioral outcome can be distinguished easily by reference to Figure 2. This figure graphically illustrates the relationships between (1) the learning process which results in learning outcomes, and (2) the responses to learning referred to as behavioral outcomes.

Close inspection of Figure 2 reveals that there should be a match between the learning outcomes or competencies that a learner is to achieve and the behavioral outcomes that are chosen as indicators of success in competency attainment. For example, if a goal is established for the achievement of a competency at the application level, Level 3.00 of the cognitive domain, then the behavioral outcome chosen as an indicator of successful competency achievement should also require a response at the application level. A competency stated at Level 5.00 would likewise require a behavioral outcome or response at Level 5.00 in competency assessment.

This same relationship exists between the learning outcomes in all three of the domains according to the hierarchical order portrayed in the cognitive, affective and psychomotor taxonomies. In other words, there should always be congruence between the learning intent or learning outcome and the behavioral response or behavioral outcome that is used to evaluate success in achieving the desired learning.

*Figure 2*

*Relationship Between Learning Outcomes (Learning)*
*and Behavioral Outcomes (Responding)*

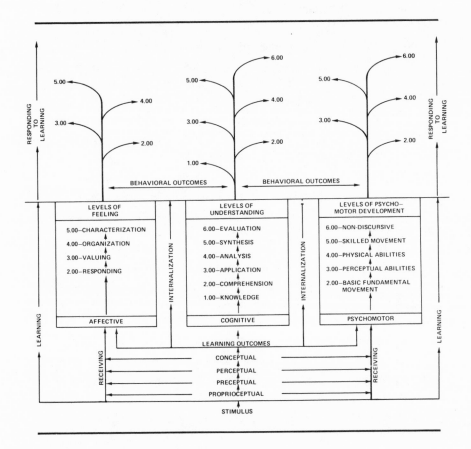

Behavioral outcomes are stated as specific performances, behavioral activities or assessment instrumentation that learners will successfully achieve as an indication that learning has occurred. In addition, a criterion is established to indicate how well the assessment activity will need to be achieved. Possible behavioral outcomes to assess student achievement of the competencies stated in the previous goal statements might be as follows:

1. Given a 20-item, short answer and multiple choice type written test, consisting of 12 selected PERT terms and eight PERT symbols, students will achieve at least 80 percent correct answers.

2. Given a PERT activity chart including a list of predecessor and successor events, the description of their corresponding activities, the average expected elapsed time for each activity, and a beginning date, students will correctly develop a written PERT control network without error in any of the data used to graphically illustrate the networks.

These two relatively simple behavioral outcome statements each contain a required performance and a criterion. In the first example, the written test is the performance while "achieving 80 percent" correct answers is the criterion. In the second example, developing a written PERT control network is the performance, whereas "doing so without error" is the criterion. One must note that these behavioral outcomes do not indicate why they are being done, what goal they will achieve, or the specific level of internalization of understanding that is being required. They are actually *assessment behaviors* which must be matched with the previously stated competencies before their value can be established.

## Behavioral Objectives: Learning
## Outcomes or Behavioral Outcomes?

Once an educator understands that the learning outcomes or competencies are not the same thing as the behavioral outcome (which are usually one-time observations of behavioral responses), he must question the value of any behavioral objective that is stated as a behavioral outcome only. This problem has caused more teacher frustration and has imperiled the behavioral objectives movement perhaps more than any other one factor.

It is not difficult to find support for this concept. In addition to Gagne (1974) and Gronlund (1974), previously mentioned, Simons (1973), Smith (1972), Harrow (1972) and others have pointed out the differences between learning outcomes and behavioral outcomes and/or the relative value of goals versus behavioral outcomes.

Currently there are two primary techniques for writing behavioral objectives. One, the "outcomes approach," implies that there is no difference between the learning outcomes (goals, competencies or learning intents) of instruction and the behavioral outcomes that students can demonstrate as evidence they have achieved the desired learning. This approach represents the work of Mager (1962) and several other early advocates of behavioral objectives as a tool of the instructional designer.

A second technique, the "goals approach," draws a distinction between learning outcomes, defined as goals, competencies or specific learning intents, and outcome behaviors that can be utilized to evaluate goal achievement. This approach is advocated by this author (1974) as well as by Harrow (1972), Gronlund (1974), Armstrong (1971) and others.

In the "outcomes approach," a behavioral objective is defined as being the behavioral outcome or performance a learner will be able to do after learning has occurred. It usually includes a behavioral activity, a criterion by which the activity can be judged and any special conditions under which the behavioral outcome must occur. In other words, the "outcomes approach" defines a behavioral objective as being simply the statement of a behavioral outcome.

In contrast, the "goals approach" defines behavioral objectives as having two components—a goal and an evaluation component. A rough analysis of these two behavioral objective writing techniques reveals that there is no essential difference between the "outcomes approach" behavioral objective and the evaluation component of the "goals approach" objective.

Substantial difference does exist, however, when the goal component is added to "goals approach" objectives. The goal, as we have previously stated, represents the only intrinsic value to be found in the instructional process and thus must be construed as being the only part of the behavioral objective to have intrinsic value. The behavioral outcome is only a means to determine success in goal achievement. Thus, any behavioral objective stated as a behavioral outcome only has nothing in it that can stand alone as being of value to the learner (aside from the fact that it represents one of many possible indicators that can be used to determine successful goal achievement).

The difference between the "goals" and "outcomes" approaches to writing behavioral objectives may be seen in Figure 3. It is obvious from Figure 3 that persons developing teaching/learning strategies for the goals approach objective will focus on achievement of the goal, and that the behavioral outcome will be considered as only one of many possible evaluation behaviors that might be sampled. On the other hand, users of the outcomes approach objective probably will develop enabling strategies to achieve only the behavioral outcomes. Thus, both the enabling strategies and the potential behavioral outcomes that *could* be used for evaluation purposes will be limited by the narrow boundaries established by the behavioral outcome statement.

Despite the agreement between the two approaches concerning the stating of the behavioral outcomes that should be exhibited at the end of a given instructional activity, the differences that do exist are conceptually incompatible. The future success or failure of the behavioral objectives and competency-based education movements (in terms of making any significant contribution to education) may depend upon the resolution and/or understanding of these differences.

Unless there is a concerted effort by institutions of higher

*Figure 3*

*A Comparison of "Goals Approach"*
*and "Outcomes Approach" Objectives*

| | GOALS APPROACH | OUTCOMES APPROACH |
|---|---|---|
| (Desired Competency or Learning Outcome) — GOAL | *Objective*:<br><br>EDU 604 students will develop the ability to write competencies as learning oriented goal statements and to apply a systems approach in the identification of instructional goals. | (No specific goal or competency required. Assumes that the behavioral outcome is its own goal.)<br><br>*Objective*:<br><br>Given the appropriate instructions, you will demonstrate your ability to graphically develop a system for identifying instructional goals, without error, and to use the system to correctly write at least five goal statements that are free from error in their communication components as outlined in the major text. |
| (Behavioral Outcome or Assessment Technique) — EVALUATION | Success will be determined by ability to graphically develop a system for identifying instructional goals, without error, and in using the system to correctly write at least five goal statements that are free from error in their communication components as outlined in the major text. | |

BEHAVIORAL OUTCOME

education and educators in general to come to some feasible agreement on what a behavioral objective should be and the functions it should serve, the real promise of the behavioral approach is unlikely to be realized. The conceptual framework within which one views a behavioral objective and the assumptions one must make according to the conceptual approach one chooses are crucial. These two choices will determine not only how objectives are written, but also how competencies are stated and evaluated, what enabling strategies will be selected to achieve the competencies, and what will ultimately be considered as the "ends" and "means" of any resulting CBE program. Are we going to utilize our enabling strategies to achieve behavioral outcomes that are merely indicators of success or are we going to develop strategies to achieve the real learning outcomes which become part of the learner?

## Economic and Political Factors

School systems and universities in general are experiencing severe financial difficulties. There is an apparent lack of confidence in educational personnel and programs. This creates distinct problems that, when added to an inflationary economy, have made people wary of many school programs and unwilling to tax themselves for school support. The public demands tight control and more accountability for the dollars invested. School bond issues are being rejected with ever increasing frequency and general school program apathy is on the increase.

The economic barriers to instructional program funding are closely tied to political barriers. School financing is contingent upon political decisions. By not supporting schools financially, citizens communicate to legislatures that they are dissatisfied. Thus, politics becomes involved in educational program planning. In addition, there are many other special interest groups who compete politically with education for top priority in funding. This is true at both the state and national levels.

Estimates have been made that the current research and

development needs of the behavioral objectives-CBE movements will require many millions of dollars. It will be difficult to obtain even a small portion of this required financial assistance for R&D within the near future. The lack of financial support can have a severe effect on both preservice and inservice education programs, a fact that may well jeopardize the behavioral objectives movement.

### National Coordination

Before any new instructional movement can be fully operationalized or implemented on a national basis, there must be some effective machinery established that will provide nationwide coordination of work efforts and problem resolution. To operationalize the behavioral objectives-CBE movements, competencies must be identified and stated in specific and valid formats. Instructional delivery systems must be prepared to enable students to better achieve the desired competencies. Assessment systems must be developed to determine program reliability and validity. Many of the current problems already identified need to be coordinated and resolved before any full-scale implementation of the movement can take place satisfactorily. For example, the controversy over the differences between a learning outcome and a behavioral outcome and the resolution of the problems created by the differences between writing behavioral objectives by the "goals" approach or "outcomes" approach are problems that could be resolved through effective national coordination. In fact, all of the problems identified in this article could be either resolved or reduced in scope and consequences if effective national coordination were available and properly funded.

### Program Assessment

A multitude of curriculum evaluation models have been submitted over the years. Many of these models have proved to be effective within the context of particular programs and with the objectives that these programs were designed to achieve. In other words, many evaluation models have been effective when viewed on a situation-specific basis. None of the evaluation models can be said to apply across-the-board to all programs. Major assessment problems in CBE include (1) the assumptions upon which CBE is based; (2) the validity and definition of competencies; (3) the certification of student performance or competency; (4) assessment of student progress, (5) assessment of teaching performance; and (6) the development of an adequate technology for performance assessment itself. To date, there appears to be little evidence that any current claims concerning behavioral objectives or CBE, either pro or con, can be supported with irrefutable program assessment evidence.

## Conclusions

Eventually, one must look at any instructional movement and make some value judgments concerning its merits. Such assessment must consider not only the movement's current status and its promise, but also the future environmental situation in which the movement must be implemented. Based upon the author's previous experience in this area, the following predictions can be made concerning the environmental context in which the behavioral objectives movement will be carved out in the future.

1. Current controversy will continue with respect to the following:
   (a) competency conceptualization and use,
   (b) whether goals should be abstract or specific,
   (c) whether competencies represent goals and specific instructional intents or behavioral outcomes,
   (d) whether competencies or behavioral outcomes are the desired program ends,
   (e) whether a learning outcome is the same thing as a behavioral outcome, and
   (f) whether behavioral outcomes are competencies or assessment techniques.
2. Economic and political factors will remain a crucial factor in

program development and implementation. Essential funding for large scale research and development efforts will not be forthcoming in amounts sufficient for properly researching and coordinating on a national basis.

3. Program assessment will remain a chief concern of many educators. A variety of new assessment models will be developed, but the minimal funding available for such efforts, along with the absence of an effective national coordination body, will prevent assessment activities from gaining wide acceptance.

4. Competency based education and performance based education will eventually be recognized by the large majority of educators as being synonymous.

5. The behavioral objectives movement will continue to grow and provide better instructional programs on a situation-specific basis. The rules of the game in producing instructional quality are the following:

    (a)  determine appropriate goals or competencies for students to achieve,

    (b)  specify effective enabling strategies and learning resources to help students achieve the desired goals, and

    (c)  evaluate student achievements to determine success.

These are precisely the factors that constitute the backbone of the behavioral objectives-CBE movement. CBE is a process that requires continuous review of desired competencies, enabling activities and evaluation procedures. Thus, CBE programs will be constantly modified for improvement and will offer new opportunities and challenges to all educators regardless of their position or expertise.

It is personal internalization and involvement that eventually brings about the success of any program. Educators become more involved and internalize change best when they are instrumental in program development and implementation within the context of the specifics of their own situation. The lack of personal involvement in the conceptualization and development of many previous movements is at least part of the reason why many previous instructional program changes have failed to produce positive results when they were transported from their development source into new environmental situations.

It is the writer's belief that the development and use of behavioral objectives will, at worst, result in some much-needed instructional program re-thinking and modification that will elevate the standards of traditional experience-based programs. At best, it will become more widespread—not a cure for all instructional program ills, but a remedy for many.

In situations where the behavioral objectives-CBE movement is properly conceptualized and implemented, it will accomplish at least the following purposes:

1. Avoid duplication in program content.

2. Prevent proliferation of course content by individual teachers.

3. Better communicate to the student the specific learning tasks that he or she should achieve.

4. Improve assessment of student achievement.

5. Aid in providing better individualization of instruction.

6. Aid in stimulation of student self-motivation.

7. Better ensure student achievement of the more complex behaviors and skills that are needed for problem solving and critical thinking.

8. Help ensure students of being able to demonstrate behaviors that are specifically related to the job functions they expect to assume in the future.

9. Improve the competencies of professional educators who develop and implement the behavioral objectives-CBE programs.

## References

Armstrong, R. *et al.* A Scheme for Evaluation. *Educational Accountability Through Evaluation*. Englewood Cliffs, New Jersey: Educational Technology Publications, 1971.

Bloom, B.S. (Ed.) *Taxonomy of Educational Objectives: Handbook I: Cognitive Domain.* New York: David McKay Company, Inc., 1956.

Gagne, R.M. Educational Technology and the Learning Process. *Educational Researcher,* January 1974, *3,* 3-8.

Gronlund, N.E. *Stating Behavioral Objectives for Classroom Instruction.* New York: The Macmillan Company, 1974, pp. 4-6.

Harrow, A.J. *A Taxonomy of the Psychomotor Domain: A Guide for Developing Behavioral Objectives.* New York: David McKay Company, Inc., 1972.

Krathwohl, D.R. *et al. Taxonomy of Educational Objectives: Handbook II, Affective Domain.* New York: David McKay Company, Inc., 1964.

Mager, R.F. *Preparing Instructional Objectives.* Palo Alto, California: Fearon Publishers, 1962.

McAshan, H.H. *The Goals Approach to Performance Objectives.* Philadelphia, Pennsylvania: W.B. Saunders Company, 1974.

Simons, H.D. Behavioral Objectives: A False Hope for Education. *Educational Digest,* April 1973, *38,* 14-16.

Smith, P.G. On the Logic of Behavioral Objectives: The Pedagogical Situation Determines Whether Objectives Should Be Precise or Vague. *Phi Delta Kappan,* March 1972, *53,* 429-431.

# 6.
# Global Behavioral Objectives:
# A Foundation for
# Teacher Freedom, Instructional Efficiency
# and Accountability

Sidney J. Drumheller

The message of this chapter is that the behavioral objective has established itself as a primary tool in providing direction, thrust and stability to the educational concerns of the school. It is obvious, of course, that an educational institution can often live at peace with its pupils and supportive community for extended periods without extensive batteries of well-defined behavioral objectives. However, when policies and programs are challenged or when conscientious, learning-oriented teachers want their role defined, the educational leadership needs the technology the behavioral objective movement has generated in order to keep its staff oriented, recall its goals and keep on course. The situation might be likened to that of a river pilot on a day liner. He can usually operate using "seat-of-the-pants" judgments, but when a fog comes in he must use the abstract language of the navigator to keep the ship on course, to defend his actions to his peers and backers, and to coordinate the efforts of his crew.

This discussion is premised on the belief that one of the major contributions that behavioral objectives technology has made is its methodology for identifying a reasonable number of measurable global behaviors for a school and then, through behavioral analysis, assigning component, teachable, subglobal behavioral objectives to individual staff members as instructional guides. Such objectives can be used to do the following:

1. Keep students and teachers accountable.

2. Provide a rationale for the delegation of instructional responsibility within an institution.
3. Keep to a minimum the restraints on a teacher by the management system.

While it is often helpful to provide an abundance of behavioral objective guidelines for a teacher who can benefit from them, it is also often best to restrict the restraints on a creative-productive teacher who is inhibited by them.

Let us begin with a definition. A behavioral objective is a statement which defines an educational goal in terms of the specific behavior demanded of a learner at a particular point in an instructional sequence. It is expected that the statement will be structured so that an informed evaluator could readily distinguish the learner who has reached the objective from the learner who has not. While curriculum designers might argue for additional restraints on the behavioral objective statement (Drumheller, 1971), the above should suffice for our purposes.

Now, let us differentiate between two (or more) levels of specificity which might alter the ends which the objectives might serve. In the training of a nurse, for instance, we might include the following objectives:

1. The graduate nurse will be judged by her patients to be compassionate, responsible and professional in her contacts with them.
2. The graduate nurse will record the diastolic and systolic blood pressures of a patient in 20 seconds using a mercurial manometer (deviating no more than three percent from the recording of a recognized expert using a similar instrument on the patient's other arm.)

Two major differences between these two objectives are obvious. The first objective is concerned with learner attitudes, while the second is concerned with skills. At the same time, and more important to this article, the first is global in nature while the second is atomistic (Drumheller, 1971).

While it is relatively easy to describe a few isolated global objectives of an instructional program, it is next to impossible to specify all the atomistic objectives which seem logically necessary to produce the global behaviors. The old humanist's axiom that "the whole is greater than the sum of its parts" seems applicable here. One cannot continue to dissect nurse-role until 100, 1,000 or 1,000,000 clean, neat, atomistic objectives (comparable to the above blood pressure objective) are generated to account for all behaviors needed by the professional nurse. Consequently, objective writers must settle for batteries of objectives which compromise the ideal of total comprehensiveness and total specificity.

The comprehensiveness factor can usually best be achieved by focusing on global behaviors defined in terms of the roles the learner will be expected to play (Drumheller, 1974). The specificity factor can usually best be achieved by focusing on clusters of teachable behaviors which identify the major portion of the role expectations (possibly 95 percent), but which are of a number that can be managed and comprehended by the educational support personnel. Unfortunately, a single set of objectives will not adequately serve most institutions because all faculty members are not able to navigate at the same level of abstraction.

Let us shift now to another objective focus—mathematics. Three sets of objectives are identified in Figure 1, any one of which might serve to support an elementary school mathematics program. The left hand column contains the first of six global and the first of sixty atomistic objectives. The center column contains one of 20 global and one of 200 atomistic objectives. The right hand column contains one of 30 global and one of 1500 atomistic objectives. The six articulated objectives identify the degree to which specificity is demanded. Remember, this chart specifies objectives for a total elementary mathematics system. Certainly, at the lesson level, the teacher is free to subdivide objectives in whatever way seems most appropriate.

Any of the three sets of objectives in Figure 1, when completed, would be considered by some educators to be both comprehensive and specific enough to meet navigational needs for charting an

## *Figure 1*

## *An Elementary School Mathematics Program*

|  | *Model I* | *Model II* | *Model III* |
|---|---|---|---|
|  | (Objectives specified at low level of articulation) | (Objectives specified at moderate level of articulation) | (Objectives specified at high level of articulation) |
| **GLOBAL OBJECTIVES** | 1. The learner will use formal mathematical processes and concepts when they are appropriate in real life situations. | 1. The learner will give evidence that he can add, subtract, multiply and divide combinations (----,----()----,----) with 95% accuracy at a rate commensurate with . . . | 1. The learner will give evidence that he can multiply a fraction by a whole number, a mixed number or another fraction with 95% accuracy at a rate commensurate with . . . |
|  | 2.6 | 2.20 | 2.30 |
| **ATOMISTIC OBJECTIVES** | 1. The learner will give evidence that he has the skills needed to transact savings, checking and loan business with a bank. | 1. The learner will give evidence that he can explain the place holding characteristic of zero and its advantage to our number system. | 1. The learner will give evidence that he can make an accurate scale drawing of a small building or land area, appropriately labeled, using a yardstick divided into 1/16 inches. Lines should be within 1/16 of what they are labeled to represent (95% accuracy required). |
|  | 2.60 | 2.200 | 2.1500 |

instructional course. That is, at a particular level of sophistication, a given battery of objectives would provide the direction and detail needed to organize and develop educational programs without inhibiting climate, creativity, etc. Different instructors require different levels of comprehensiveness and specificity.

The Gagnes, the Magers, the Pophams and others have been arguing for over a decade that objective writers should use their particular models for determining the specificity of objectives. In reality, however, most functioning educational units attempting such puristic pursuits end up with a complex of objectives that is unique to a particular institution and that is often unrecognizable as a relative of the model which gave it birth.

Herbert Simon coined the term "satisfice" to represent the compromise position that business management settles for when it attempts to institute a designed institutional change and meets resistance from certain factions. The author of this article takes the position that the leadership in an educational enterprise must see to it that the institution serves its constituents by efficiently nurturing the global behaviors it espouses. While some educators need highly detailed batteries of objectives, others do not and are actually frustrated by such specificity. A single set of highly detailed behavioral objectives can be frightening, repulsive and inhibiting. If a faculty could be given several compatible sets of objectives from which individuals could select, the subsequent instruction would result in a "satisfice condition" much closer to the initial design than if a single set of objectives were mandated. In other words, Simon's satisfice state will be much closer to the ideal state if alternate batteries of behavioral objectives, with which an institution expects a teacher to identify, could be roughly tailored to the skills, temperament and teaching style of the teacher-navigators. This could be accomplished if the terminal global objectives were mandated, and alternative sets of global objectives, varying in detail, were available to suit the abstract-concrete cognitive style of individual teachers. Three such sets of objectives for a mathematics sequence were suggested in Figure 1.

Other suggestions for global objectives in communications, social development and self development are presented elsewhere (Drumheller, 1972b).

### Three Types of
### Institutional Climate

Let us focus our attention for a moment on three climates which exist in any public educational institution—a political climate, a school-playing climate and an educational climate. Here, the term climate refers to a prevailing set of attitudes held in common by members of an institution which tend to determine both the morale of the members and their readiness to respond to particular problem situations within the institution.

Figure 2 depicts the administrator and the teacher within a school struggling to stabilize the three climates so that the institution can best reach its goals. An interesting problem arises, however, because conditions force both administrator and teacher to give particular climates priorities. A threatening political climate captures the administrator's attention while a segment of the teacher's class, unwilling to play the game of school, captures the teacher's attention. The learning climate is then put on the back-burner to fend for itself while the teacher and the administrator tend to more pressing matters.

"Political climate" is usually generated by organized groups within the school or community demanding changes in policy or conditions within the school. Such groups apply their pressure either directly at the administrator level or indirectly through the school board. Often the administrator views one of his roles as that of a protector—a protector of the teacher from political pressure. In such a situation, only the administration feels the full effect of the pressure. Teachers feel only the effects of the administrator's reaction and probably feel little or no compulsion to try to solve the political problems of the administrator.

"School-playing climate" results from the interaction of the teacher and pupils in the classroom. Teachers usually feel that

*Figure 2*

*The Climatic Concers of Administrator
and Teacher: An Institutional Reality*

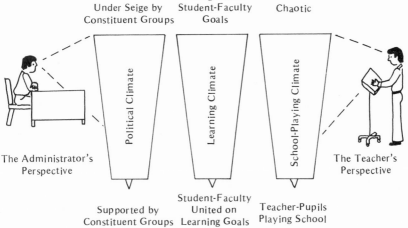

COUNTER-PRODUCTIVE ELEMENTS

Under Seige by     Antagonistic
Constituent Groups   Student-Faculty    Chaotic
             Goals

Political Climate    Learning Climate    School-Playing Climate

The Administrator's                             The Teacher's
Perspective                                     Perspective

               Student-Faculty
Supported by       United on     Teacher-Pupils
Constituent Groups   Learning Goals   Playing School

SUPPORTIVE ELEMENTS

Only when outside climates are stabilized can internal climate be observed and nurtured.

they can concentrate on the fine points of the learning environment only after the learners agree to come to class on time, sit in their seats when so requested, follow directions, participate in class activities, raise their hands to speak, etc. (Drumheller, 1972a). As an administrator is expected to maintain a peaceful, cooperative climate with his staff, pupils and community, so a teacher is expected to maintain at least a traditional school-playing climate in the classroom. While varying teacher competencies in maintaining a supportive learning climate are tolerated, all teachers are expected to maintain a basic school-playing climate.

The "learning-climate" is distinct from the two climates just discussed. The image of students diligently pursuing their individual objectives, with the total complement of faculty, ready, willing and able to facilitate that pursuit, portrays a school climate that would warm the hearts of the vast majority of educators in the late 1970s. This learning climate would be charted along a continuum, one end of which would depict an absence of commitment on the part of learners and faculty to the school's learning programs and goals, and the other end of which would depict a total united commitment to the same.

Thus, Figure 2 is intended to demonstrate the remoteness of the learning climate from the front line concerns of both the teacher and administrator. "Happiness" tends to be defined by the administrator in terms of the peacefulness of the political climate, and by the teacher in terms of the peacefulness of the school-playing climate. When the air clears and the all-important learning climate is visible, it can be tended to by those who are so inclined. Unfortunately, hyperactive lobbyists and bouncing pupils keep the administrator and teacher in the political and school-playing games. In many schools the concern for learning climate tends to get central office consideration only occasionally at formal events such as a faculty pep rally or an inservice training day.

There is a game played with tops called "keep the pot boiling" where each player is supposed to keep three tops spinning continuously. When two of a player's tops lose their momentum, he or she loses the game. Unfortunately, or perhaps fortunately, it is difficult to tell when the "learning top" stops in a classroom. As just pointed out, there is often no one watching it closely because most schools do not have an effective system for monitoring the educational climate and the learning process. A system of behavioral objectives can provide a structural framework for giving the school and teacher the needed direction and stability to stay on course during foul weather, and the assurance that the educational role as well as the school-playing and political roles of the school will be attended to. Further discussion of the climate objectives demanded by a school community is available elsewhere (Drumheller, 1972a).

### Global Objectives as a Tool for
### Building an Effective Educational Climate

When administrators are held accountable for the equitable apportionment of global behavioral objectives to the staff of a school, as well as for the monitoring of the instructional programs focused on these objectives, and when teachers are held account-able for the scheduling of instructional programs to reach these objectives and the rallying of pupils around these objectives, then sufficient pot-watchers are available to keep vigil over the educational climate of the school. All of the interested parties—principals, teachers, students and parents—can be instrumental in the process of keeping the program goal-centered and successful. While 2000 to 3000 atomistic behavioral goals secreted away by the teacher can be as easily ignored as the vague platitudes of old, the 25 to 50 global behavioral objectives expected of a learner during a given year can be easily policed by a child's grandmother or the next-door neighbor.

Implied in this global approach is the belief that the behaviors needed by a child can be clustered into meaningful categories and then sub-divided into specific behavioral roles that the learner is expected to play. There are certainly many possible patterns for such divisions. For over 2000 years we have built curricula around the seven liberal arts. Figure 3 portrays the Roman version, the 20th century American version and a behavioral version which now seems to be emerging. While the traditional subject-centered instruction with its diversified academic thrusts makes the problem of defining global objectives difficult, the newer, cross-discipline, functional organizational patterns tend to simplify the task.

The four emerging behavioral clusters illustrated in Figure 3 can be adopted in existing school systems with only minor changes in perspective, once the global behavioral objective orientation is assumed. The "self actualizing" core is given to the social studies and humanities staff; the "communications" core to the speech, composition and reading staff; the "mathematical tools" core to the mathematics staff; and the "physical world coping" core to the science staff. The next step would be to subdivide the cores into behavioral roles and the roles into developmental levels.

The author has developed such a scheme for use in general education (1972b). This scheme was developed because it is compatible with the existing academic competencies of today's educators. Many other equally valid schemes could be devised, but this is sufficient to illustrate the fact that the leap from the traditional to global behavioral clusters can be taken without major organizational change or risk-taking. It does imply, however, that many isolated, nice-to-know objectives in our present curriculum should either be linked to a need-to-know global objective or set adrift to be picked up by the learner in his day-to-day living.

**The Status of the Art of**
**Instructional Navigation**

Prior to the advent of Sputnik, curricula throughout America were rather standardized and stable. National professional education groups made periodic recommendations regarding curricular modifications, which in turn were endorsed by the separate states and sharply defined by the texts distributed by the nation's publishers.

*Figure 3*

*Teachable Behavioral Clusters from
the Seven Liberal Arts*

| *The Seven Liberal Arts of Ancient Rome:* | *20th Century Subjects Evolving from the Liberal Arts:* | *Behavioral Clusters Evolving from the Liberal Arts Tradition:* |
|---|---|---|
| Music | Music, Art | Self Actualizing Perceptions and Skills (Including Social) |
| Grammar | Grammar, Literature History, Mythology | |
| Rhetoric | Rhetoric | Communication Skills |
| Dialectics | Logic | |
| Arithmetic | Arithmetic, Algebra | Using Mathematical Tools |
| Geometry | Geometry, Trigonometry | |
| Astronomy | Botony, Zoology, Astronomy, Physics, Chemistry, Mechanics | Coping in the Physical World |

Government educational pump-priming activities geared to helping us catch up with the Russians has flooded the schools with innovative programs, personnel, materials and monies that have broken our lockstep patterns but also have created what some educators have called the era of non-curriculum. While two decades ago the nation's educational ship could be likened to a single armada, it is now composed of two million teachers in separate lifeboats (or individual atomic submarines, if you wish). While teachers formerly tended to be timid followers of a dictatorial administrator, they now tend to be imaginative, courageous captains of their own small ships.

This state of affairs has positive as well as negative ramifications. Let us consider some positive aspects first.

1. Teachers now have both the will and freedom to focus on the individual needs of the students and to attack the educational objectives they deem important.
2. Many teachers are demonstrating that they can build and refine curricula using their own resources within their own classrooms.
3. The public image of the teacher is changing from that of a docile subservient individual to that of an aggressive, professional learning facilitator who works as a clinician to meet the needs of his or her charges.

Some negative effects of this era of non-curriculum include the following:

1. The old scope and sequence charts have disappeared, eliminating the rationale for assigning educational goals to various instructional sequences and to various levels in instructional sequences.
2. The newly emerging, self-sufficient, independent teacher is no longer expected to respond to decrees from above with respect to complex or arbitrary scope and sequence demands.
3. While highly abstract management systems can be communicated in a series of inservice workshops, their documents tend to be too complex to be remembered and used by the average teacher.

Over the last two decades, teachers have developed their own private curricula. A few have carefully charted their instructional programs and can defend their components and rationales. However, they often cannot communicate to their colleagues what they are doing and how they can support each other because they lack the navigational language.

Teachers are truly in a bind. They have finally achieved a professional level of independence from authority. They are accumulating substantive evidence of their success in the new role. On the other hand, they recognize some of the advantages of the old order (an order that the systematic use of behavioral objectives might restore). They dislike the ambiguities in the new "open" education, but they fear that they might lose more than they gain by aligning themselves with another Messianic system—especially the behavioral objective system that let so many of them down less than a decade ago.

Commercially prepared, printed instructional materials have provided the fabric of instructional programs for two centuries. Behavioral objectives enthusiasts argue that the published material focus should be replaced by the objective focus. They insist that a labyrinth of statements should replace the colorful, fascinating, concrete packages of "goodies" that are dangled before teachers' eyes by salesmen or placed on their desks by administrators. This wholesale switch is not likely to occur in the near future. A behavioral objective based navigational system that is capable of implementation must be far more global and more easily comprehensible to the typical teacher than anything yet devised. It must be functional as a tool for the following purposes:

(1)   in selecting new instructional materials,
(2)   in selecting the innovational waves to be ridden,
(3)   in evaluating pupil progress regardless of materials being used,
(4)   in delegating responsibilities within an instructional unit (probably a building) or between instructional units, and
(5)   as a tool that will remain intact (essentially) throughout successive curricular changes.

Currently, the "art of instructional navigation" is truly an art to most of the profession, although educational technologists have the rudiments on which a rational (scientific) system can be built. Efforts to implement educational management systems have had limited success and have focused typically on a single innovative program. The average teacher in an open setting must devise his or her own navigational art form and accompanying skills. Instructional navigation is learned by the individual teacher as his or her students and colleagues modify that teacher's behavior with a variety of awards and punishments.

Administrators and teachers desperately need navigational tools to tell them where they have been, where they currently are and where they should be headed. They need tools at their level of sophistication that also are compatible with those used by their colleagues. The fleshing out of objective batteries similar to those depicted in Figure 1 could provide the needed guidelines.

As a ship's captain cannot spend 24 hours a day at the helm, with his eyes glued to the horizon, neither can a teacher devote full time to policing objectives. Behavioral technologists of the last decade have established that objectives posted along navigation routes serve well to chart the way to the reaching of the complex global behaviors needed by the learner in coping with his world. The time it takes to attend to the channel is minimal and the assurance that one has that he is on course is gratifying. While the profession has not yet agreed upon the management system for policing the behavioral objective system, a procedure has been verified for marking the channel.

### The Ideal Role of Behavioral
### Objectives in Today's School

In defining a realistic perspective regarding the role of behavioral objectives in education, the following four seemingly conflicting generalizations must be understood and brought into balance:

1. Exhaustive lists of atomistic, educational objectives have a frustrating and inhibiting effect on a faculty and are of little use to either teacher or administrator.

2. Teachers and administrators are expected to be able to play the roles both of humanist and technologist at the same time.
3. No institution can afford to be without a blueprint of behavioral objectives which specifies the functional educational role each member of the instructional and administrative staff is expected to play.
4. No institution can afford to be without leaders and teachers skilled in the science of objective writing, analysis and management.

Now let us look separately at each of these apparently conflicting generalizations.

*Exhaustive lists of atomistic objectives are useless.* Efforts over the past decade to identify every "nice to know" fact, term, generalization, etc., that is referred to within an instructional program, and to convert these to comprehensive sets of behavioral objectives, has proven to be an exercise in futility. When a person writes notes to remind himself to do certain things, he strives to be both brief and comprehensive at the same time. He would seldom make a list to remind himself to put on his trousers and shoes before leaving for work. When compiling objectives for a unit, course or sequence, one should strive for elegance. The list should have the right mix of specificity and generality to maximize its utilitarian value. As was mentioned above, it might be wise to provide two or three parallel lists which vary in specificity from which the teacher could choose.

*A teacher must be helped to be both a humanist and a technologist.* Contemporary employers demand that the teacher reflect in his interactions with his pupils an understanding of their wants and needs, and a compassion for them as they wrestle with failures, frustrations, tedium, boredom and success. At the same time, he or she is a professional and is expected to use the technological tools of the profession which have proven their worth in the educational process. There are situations where the serving of these two masters at the same time seems next to impossible. Occasionally, one has to be sacrificed for the other, but this should be infrequent. A teacher should be held accountable for professional shortcomings in either direction. Unreasonable administrative pressures to force the non-analytic teacher toward a rigid, technological innovation can transform the teacher into a robot. Monstrous and incomprehensible behavioral objective systems can be dehumanizing. At the same time, there is no better educational or developmental guidance system than one organized around global behavioral objectives. Educational leaders must nurture a curricular management system which allows maximum flexibility for the humanistic qualities of the teacher to emerge, just as the guidance system should provide maximum behavioral growth for the learner. A healthy educational climate can be maintained within and supported by a behavioral objective navigation system if it can be adjusted to the analytic, intuitive thinking styles of the individual teachers in the system (Drumheller, 1970, 1973).

*Every school needs navigational charts based on behavioral objectives.* In the preceding discussion on climates, it was emphasized that educational goals and climate are often forgotten when school staffs are preoccupied with political and school-playing concerns. In our present era of non-curriculum, where syllabi and textbook series are short lived, the individual teacher is the prime coordinator of educational programs for the developing child under his or her supervision. We now have the technology for becoming far more efficient in the accomplishment of our educational task, without sacrificing our humanistic gains. Such navigational charts can be built within the following parameters:

1. Most of the global behaviors needed by the learner (either as a child or as an adult) can be identified for faculty, community and learners.
2. Faculty, community and learners can identify those global behaviors for which the *school* can be held responsible.
3. A master plan should be devised assigning responsibility for the development of these behaviors among grades, departments, or groups of grades and departments. Where responsi-

bility for a global behavior cannot be assigned, it will be necessary to analyze it and break it down into teachable components.

4. Negotiations between the instructional staff and the community (or its school board representatives) will have to take place to establish a "satisficial" contractual relationship wherein the instructional personnel agree to work as a team to reach the community educational goals.

5. Intelligible navigational charts can then be constructed to rally community, administration, teacher and student support for the educational task of the school so that a goal-centered educational climate can be sustained.

Such a thrust will give the total educational community direction and will provide a means by which teachers, administrators and students can be held accountable for their performances.

## References

Drumheller, S.J. Verbal and Nonverbal Knowledge in Curriculum Development and Teaching. *Educational Technology*, November 1970, *10*, 19-24.

Drumheller, S.J. *Handbook of Curriculum Design for Individualized Instruction: A Systems Approach.* Englewood Cliffs, New Jersey: Educational Technology Publications, 1971.

Drumheller, S.J. Curriculum Making as a Game Designing Task. *Educational Technology*, May 1972a, *12*, 13-17.

Drumheller, S.J. *Teacher's Handbook for a Functional Behavior-Based Curriculum: Communicable Models and Guides for Classroom Use.* Englewood Cliffs, New Jersey: Educational Technology Publications, 1972b.

Drumheller, S.J. Competency Based Instruction Systems and the Human Facilitators: Confessions of a Module Writer. *Educational Technology*, April 1973, *13*, 9-13.

Drumheller, S.J. Competency Based Teacher Education Must Emphasize Fewer and More Global Behaviors to Maximize Efficiency and Morale. *Educational Technology*, March 1974, *14*, 3-11.

# 7.
# The Competency-Based Movement: Origins and Future

W. Robert Houston and
Allen R. Warner

Perhaps no movement in recent years has so captured the imagination of American educators as has competency-based education. In less than a decade it has pressed both strong advocates and equally strong detractors to define more precisely what is meant by "education." Such precision in definition has been greatly aided, of course, by the behavioral objectives movement. First applied to teacher education,* the competency-based movement has spread to other areas of education including pre-college programs, vocational job training and other professions. It has been employed as a way to insure minimum levels of achievement by high school graduates, as a process for certifying teachers, and in a myriad of other ways. In all of this activity, competency-based education has become political as well as educational.

## Essence of CBE

In many ways, competency-based education reflects the basic tenets of American society with respect to ·its pragmatic concern for *doing*, not just *knowing how to do*, and with continuing to do that which appears to be effective in achieving objectives.

---

*The ten elementary models for teacher preparation supported by the Bureau of Research, USOE, in 1968-69 are typically credited as the epoch for competency-based education. See B. Joyce. *EPDA and Competency Based Education.* Palo Alto: Stanford Center for Research and Development in Teaching, 1975.

Ultimately, competence is judged on the basis of results—on accomplishments that are the consequences of actions.

Competency-based teacher education is a term coined initially by advocates of a movement which sought to base teacher education on behaviorally stated objectives related to teacher effectiveness. Such objectives would be explicit, public and directly linked to teacher roles. Instructional activities would relate directly to such objectives. Assessment criteria and program requirements would be explicitly affected by such objectives. As the movement spread, definitions proliferated and the concept broadened to embrace many positions and theories (AACTE, 1974; Elam, 1972; Houston, 1974; and Rosner and Kay, 1974). Somewhere in all this activity the essence of the movement became entangled with other movements and concepts (e.g., modular instruction, open education, behaviorism, criterion-referenced assessment and field-based preparation).

While names for the movement have varied widely, two are prominently employed—competency-based education (CBE) and performance-based education (PBE). Names sometimes include role descriptions, as in competency-based teacher education (CBTE) and performance-based administrator education (PBAE). As pointed out in the following quotation (Houston, 1972), the names applied to this movement reflect the important characteristics of it:

> Advocates of "performance-based" terminology refer to the *way in which teachers demonstrate teaching knowledge and skills.* That demonstration is observable (and their objectives are to "write," "do," "describe," not "understand" or "perceive" which are non-observable). Further, performance reminds us that knowledge of content and teaching strategies is not sufficient in teaching—overt action is important.
>
> "Competency-based" emphasizes a *minimum standard*; it adds criterion levels, value orientations and quality to the definition of the movement. While competency advocates note three levels for criteria—cognitive, performance, and consequence—they press for the latter as the most significant measure of effectiveness. Performance advocates, also recognizing consequence as the ultimate test of an individual's effectiveness, point out that many intervening variables affect results (pupil ability, interest, motivation, availability of resources). They stress that our present

understanding of these variables and our inability to control them adequately in field settings preclude consequence objectives as realistic requirements. Thus, objectives requiring performance become the major ones in a teacher preparation program, and performance-based is more descriptive as a generic name for this movement.

Both performance-based and competency-based express important elements of the movement—one focusing on objectives, the other on criteria (pp. 25-26).

Both human nature and the preponderance of research indicate that persons are generally more likely to achieve clearly delineated goals and objectives than fuzzy or unknown ones. A review of research on incidental and intentional learning (Duchastel and Merrill, 1973) and on mastery learning (Block, 1971) identified the wide range of research findings in this area. Although several studies failed to find significant relationships between student achievement and student knowledge of objectives, the preponderance of research confirmed the hypothesis that students who know the specific objectives of instruction achieve more than those unaware of the objectives. (Dawley and Dawley, 1974; Duchastel and Brown, 1975; Hauck and Thomas, 1972; Morse and Tellman, 1972; Rothkopf and Kaplan, 1972; and Wolk, 1973).

Building on research on intentional and mastery learning, CBE made two important additions. First, objectives were based on the required and optimal behaviors of practicing professionals. Second, knowledge alone was not considered to be adequate; competency-based programs focused primarily on *performance* and the *consequence* of behaviors. The first addition actually involved the *validity* issue in professional education. Programs not rooted in the required and optimal behaviors of practitioners risked irrelevant training objectives and programs. The second addition reminded professional educators that knowledge of content was not adequate; performance and the consequences of performance were to be the critical criteria for judging professional behavior. *It became far more important, for example, that teachers were able to teach and to bring about change in their students rather than simply to "know about" teaching.* Such a stance does not, of course, diminish the importance of knowledge nor the relationship among knowledge, decisioning and performance.

Competencies identify a conceptual frame for the professional. While providing the basis for preparation programs, competencies usually are translated into more specific objectives for instructional purposes. Competencies differ from behavioral objectives in several ways. For example, as these terms are typically used, competencies: (1) are logically derived from a role conception; (2) are broader in scope; (3) define programs rather than instructional unit outcomes; (4) require multiple assessments to accommodate varied contexts, criteria and conditions; (5) emphasize performance and consequences of actions over cognitive outcomes (while behavioral objectives may relate equally well to any one of these three); and (6) are oriented typically toward professional or vocational roles.

### Extensiveness of the Movement

Conference programs, professional dialogues and current publications indicate that many institutions are engaged in competency-based programs. The actual extent to which CBE is being implemented probably cannot be known, but the data suggest that it is extensive and growing. For example, in 1971 Schmieder listed 22 items on the subject in his first bibliography, and 800 items three years later (Schmieder, 1974, p. 368). By 1976, Cappuzzello (1976) had identified over 6,000 items.

In 1972, the American Association of Colleges for Teacher Education conducted a survey of 1200 institutions preparing teachers, asking if they were operating, investigating and/or planning competency-based teacher education programs (Schmieder, 1972). Of the 783 respondents (a 65 percent return), 131 (17 percent) said they were operating CBTE programs, 228 (29 percent) said they were not, and a large number, 424 (54 percent), said they were in some stage of exploration and study.

In May 1973, Educational Testing Service in conjunction with AACTE made a follow-up survey of the 131 institutions that had identified themselves in the initial survey as having competency-based programs (Sherwin, 1974). Seventy-five useable responses were received. A large proportion of the respondents, 71 percent (53 institutions), had operated CBTE programs less than two years. Most of the CBE activity was reported at the undergraduate level. According to the returns, a total of 24,399 students were engaged in CBE programs.

In 1975, Westbrook and Sandefur (1975) surveyed member institutions in AACTE to determine the extent to which they were involved in CBTE. Of the 865 AACTE members, 570 (66 percent) returned the survey. Of these, 288 institutions (52 percent) indicated they were operating CBTE programs. This compared with 17 percent operating CBTE programs in 1972. Only 17 percent were not involved in CBTE programs in 1975 as contrasted with 29 percent three years earlier. While ten institutions reported full-scale CBTE programs in 1972, 47 did so in 1975. Westbrook and Sandefur (1975) concluded that "(1) institutions are continuing to move toward some CBTE model; and (2) areas most frequently involved by CBTE institutions are elementary education, secondary education, special education, and educational psychology" (p. 277).

According to Pittman (1975), during the past five years *every state* has *studied* CBE/Competency-Based Certification. Twenty-six states have revised their teacher education and certification standards, with all revisions resulting in "approved program approaches." Of the 29 states utilizing the approved program approach, 17 either have developed separate CBTE standards or were encouraging CBE program development through the approved program approach. Twenty-three states have produced documents which specifically address either competency-based education or competency-based certification.

At the federal level, several programs that highlight CBE approaches include the Teacher Corps, the Fund for the Improvement of Post Secondary Education, and Career Education. The National Council on Education Professions Development (1976), established to review EPDA federal programs, recently recommended continued study of CBE (p. 19).

CBE approaches have surfaced at the international level also. The Free University of Iran will open in 1978 as a completely competency-based university. Teachers colleges in Israel, Saudi Arabia and Australia are studying CBE. UNESCO sponsored a week-long training conference in 1973 for its chief technical advisors from around the world. An innovative project in technical education operates in Munich and one on basic education functions in Brazil.

While originating in professional education as a movement to prepare teachers, CBE also has spread to many other fields. Among CBE professional programs are The University of Texas Dental School, Antioch School of Law in Washington, D.C., the College of Human Services in New York City, and the doctoral program in management at Case Western Reserve. Alverno College in Milwaukee has established a competency-based liberal arts degree. The Contemporary Learning Center, a high school in Houston for drop-outs, successfully employs CBE principles in its program. The state of Oregon recently established exit competencies for awarding high school diplomas. Among major corporations, McDonald's trains restaurant managers, and Shell Oil trains refinery operators by this approach.

## Criticisms of Competency-Based Education

Criticisms of CBE have focused on its effect on the teaching profession, the possibility of its use or misuse by cunning or naive people, and on the impracticality of the approach. Some criticisms are derived from conceptual differences while others reflect political positions.

The National Council on Education Professions Development (1976) distinguished CBE theory from practice, as follows:

> The simplicity of the idea, which is based on input-output analysis of tasks, is in contrast to the actual difficulty of doing it. Specifying competencies for certain jobs, developing methods to teach them, and measuring the effectiveness of the teaching methods used, are extremely complicated activities (p. 4).

Haynes and Coyne (1971) were concerned that competencies would perpetuate the status quo in schools. Since teachers would be judged on current standards of performance in classrooms, they might forsake more innovative and newer approaches. Hogan (1973) was concerned that instructional skills could be conceptualized as isolated from content. Broudy (1974) distinguished the *performer* (actor) from the *professional who performs*, and was concerned that the CBE emphasis on performance would lead to actions without an undergirding conceptual base. Tarr (1974) supported Broudy's position in the following statement: "Performance as an isolated factor is not as accurate a reflection of a person's ability as might appear. Variables such as the classroom itself, years of teaching, sex, etc., are factors that will influence actual performance on the job" (p. 85).

Some critics (Tarr, 1974; and Merrow, 1974) have been concerned about integrating teaching competencies into what Bruce Joyce has referred to as a "seamless web of teaching." Broudy (1972) accused CBE proponents of assuming that the teaching act was merely the sum of performances into which it was analyzed.

Assessment of competence has repeatedly been noted as a major weakness of CBE. In an early document on the subject, Elam (1972) stated that: "The overriding problem before which the others pale to insignificance is that of the adequacy of measurement instruments and procedures" (p. 3). McDonald (1974) considered the implications of this problem:

> The lack of a substantial scientific foundation to support the choice of teaching skills to be learned does not mean that professional educators or teachers themselves have no ideas as to the relevant competencies needed in teaching. There is a rich, if not over abundant, literature on teaching and teaching skills. But the concepts, theories, and hypotheses about teaching skills

necessary to produce certain desirable changes in pupils are
largely untested. To say that they are untested does not mean
that the ideas are worthless, only that their validity remains to be
demonstrated.

Many professional organizations and learned societies have
considered the impact of CBE (Massanari, 1975) and have reacted
to the movement in a variety of ways. Scarcely a professional
conference has been held in the past four years without CBE as a
program topic. Committees have been appointed and position
papers written. The National Education Association condemned
CBE as being premature in a 1974 resolution passed by its General
Assembly. The American Federation of Teachers supported CBE
while condemning certification based on such processes. Social
science and humanities associations typically have opposed the
movement, while more technically oriented associations have
supported it or remained silent on the issue. Merrow (1974)
summarized the political struggle as follows: "Although one would
not know it from reading educational journals, the movement to
reform teacher training is part of a political struggle between
increasingly militant teachers and those who have traditionally
exercised control over public education" (p. 11).

## The Promise

The controversy and discussion surrounding competency-based
education over the past decade has had a maturing effect on the
movement. Presently competency-based education seems to be in
an adolescent stage, promising power that has yet to be fully
demonstrated. While theoretically sound, CBE is yet to be fully
implemented in any program. The programs now underway are
only approximations of CBE in action. Whether that promised
power comes to mature fruition depends on correcting some of
the inadequacies identified by early adopters and by early critics
of CBE. The future of CBE may well be linked to its development
in three areas—new bases for specifying competencies, linking
training procedures with outcome specifications, and competency

assessment. Each of these areas is discussed in the following paragraphs.

*Competency Specifications.* To date, virtually all competency lists have been derived from *a priori* perceptions of practitioners or teacher educators. Their limitations in vision, personal perceptual screens and the lore of past programs have all limited the potential for more relevant and more effective approaches to competency specification.

Individual conceptions of competent behaviors have been pooled by program designers and delineated as competency statements. Such statements are, in reality, *indications of competence* which typically include only the more obvious indicators of competence. Designers may not recognize, or be able to verbalize, some elements of competence. In pooling the perceptions of many people, something is lost in the process of negotiating the wording of statements. Language seems to limit the translation of mental conceptions to written statements so that written specifications are never quite so adequate as the unverbalized conceptual model of global competence that each participant has brought to the task.

The initial conceptualization of competency-based education included the notion of developing competencies from an empirical research base on teaching. A decade ago, however, precious little was available to provide that empirical base. Much that had been written about teaching methodology abounded with professional folklore and conventional wisdom rather than research findings.

While still meager, there now exists a growing body of empirical studies on teacher effectiveness. In November 1975, a National Conference on Teacher Effectiveness was held at The University of Texas-Austin at which a number of significant papers were delivered.* Most of these research studies were limited, however, to mathematics and reading at the elementary level. Clearly, one

*Many of those papers were summarized in the Spring 1976 issue of the *Journal of Teacher Education* (27, No. 1).

of the major challenges of competency-based education is to move from the conventional wisdom-consensus model for competency specification to an empirically derived, data-based model.

Another challenge in competency specification is to increase the breadth of operationally defined competencies to include affective qualities such as empathy, openness, flexibility, creativity and perseverance. While generally espoused as important for most professionals, these areas are usually not included in preparation program specifications.

*Program-Outcome Linkage.* Once competency statements have been developed (by whatever model), the next challenge is to link those outcome statements directly and systematically with training practices and procedures. Too many programs today include well-worded and well-intended competencies that bear little or no relationship either to training program activities or to criterion requirements for program completion. Prospective teachers, for example, have been taught about individualizing instruction while sitting in large group lectures.

Our point here is neither new nor innovative but one that has been made many times by other writers—and often ignored or neglected by implementers of competency-based education. Unless program activities are carefully and systematically interfaced with specified competencies, educators are operating no differently from a golf pro who gives his clients only a book to read and then expects them to drive a ball 250 yards as a final examination.

*Assessment of Competency Demonstration.* Competency demonstration is a complex of personal and situational attributes. In its latest funding of competency-based research, the National Institute of Education specified both skill and situation parameters. While generic competencies applicable to all persons in a particular role will continue to be identified, situational parameters will probably lead to the generation of banks of behavioral indicators of competence that can be applied in situation-specific contexts. The interaction and interdependence among competencies and between competencies and other variables (e.g., personal characteristics, social and environmental characteristics, instructional areas, resource base, etc.) will be considered in developing such banks.

Traditional data collection instruments and procedures will require further refinement. Current observation instruments tend to be time consuming, inadequate, and often not valid reflections of the competency behaviors they are supposed to sample. Before research on competency demonstration can proceed very far, more adequate instruments must be developed. In practice, instrument design and research utilizing those instruments should progress as a tandem development.

Criterion levels for competency demonstration will increasingly be studied. Up to this point, the assumption has been roughly that "more is better." Several studies, however, have demonstrated that some relationships are curvilinear, and that one may "know too much" or "be too skilled" in some specific areas for the role requirements of teaching. Soar (1973) summarized several studies which examined the relationships between teacher indirectness and pupil growth in measures which were complex and abstract; simple and concrete; and intermediate between those two extremes. His analysis showed a linear relationship between indirectness and pupil growth *only* for complex, abstract measures. As pupil measures became more simple and more concrete, higher levels of teacher indirectness were less productive.

We recognize that more is not necessarily better in the quantity of food consumed, the amount of exercise engaged in, the amount of money spent on a particular project or the amount of open affection shown by a mother for her child. Up to a certain extent, more in each example leads to better outcomes, but as the amount becomes excessive, the effects become negative rather than positive.

So it may be with many teaching competencies. Not only must the profession consider the nature of competencies required; it must also examine the relative effects of various criterion levels.

## Conclusion

In a very short time as educational innovations go, competency-based education has become recognized world-wide as an
important educational movement—praised for its promise, damned
for its shortcomings, and tested in a wide variety of settings with
programs based on varied theoretical constructs.

The mass of written materials on competency-based education
grows daily, most of it published in the past five years. Much that
has been written is redundant—but it does reflect increased power
in the movement, development of less rigid systems, evolving
creativity of approaches, increasing dependence on a growing body
of research, extension of CBE to consider setting variables, and a
growing number of persons who have just discovered CBE.

Less than a decade ago the term "competency-based education"
had yet to be coined. CBE developed, however, out of strong
historic and social roots in education, the professions and
American culture. Needs for relevance in teacher education, the
contemporary focus on innovation, and an established emphasis
on behavioral objectives all pressed for new and vital approaches.

Predicting the specific nature of competency-based education a
decade from now is difficult. Very likely the name will have
changed; for many people competency-based education has
become what S.I. Hayakawa has called a "code-word"—a term that
engenders emotional connotations, either highly positive or highly
negative, depending on the predisposition and life experience of
the perceiver. However, the basic concepts of CBE and their
residual effects will continue to be felt for many years. Competency-based education offers a process for directly addressing many
major and persistent educational issues. Among those issues are:
"What is the real meaning of the myriad of paper credentials our
society issues so readily and values so highly?" "How can the skills
and experience be measured that individuals bring with them to a
learning environment?" "When is a teacher—or lawyer, physician
or plumber—competent?" The CBE movement will continue to
draw strength from extended vigorous research on effective

professional practice, on efficient training programs and on useful assessment instruments and practices.

## References

American Association of Colleges for Teacher Education, Committee on Performance-Based Teacher Education. *Achieving the Potential of Performance-Based Teacher Education: Recommendations.* Washington, D.C.: AACTE, 1974.

Block, J.H. (Ed.) *Mastery Learning: Theory and Practice.* New York: Holt, Rinehart and Winston, 1971.

Broudy, H.S. *A Critique on Performance-Based Teacher Education.* Washington, D.C.: American Association of Colleges for Teacher Education, 1972.

Broudy, H.S. Why Oppose CBTE? In W.R. Houston, *Exploring Competency-Based Education.* Berkeley, Calif.: McCutchan, 1974, 58-65.

Cappuzzello, P.G. Personal letter dated August 11, 1976, describing the work of the Academic Development Resource Center, Bowling Green State University in annotating CBE documents.

Dawley, L.T. and H.H. Dawley. Incidental and Intentional Learning of Economic Information in Beginning Typewriting. *Perceptual and Motor Skills,* 1974, *38,* 337-338.

Duchastel, P.C. and B.R. Brown. Incidental and Relevant Learning with Instructional Objectives. *Journal of Educational Psychology,* 1975, *66,* 481-485.

Duchastel, P.C. and P.F. Merrill. The Effects of Behavioral Objectives on Learning: A Review of Empirical Studies. *Review of Educational Research,* 1973, *43,* 53-69.

Elam, S. *Performance-Based Teacher Education: What Is the State of the Art?* Washington, D.C.: American Association of Colleges for Teacher Education, 1972.

Hauck, W.E. and J.W. Thomas. The Relationship of Humor to Intelligence, Creativity and Intentional and Incidental Learning. *Journal of Experimental Education,* Summer 1972, *40,* 52-54.

Haynes, S.E. and C.E. Coyne. Accountability in Teacher Education. *Bulletin of the National Association of Secondary School Principals,* December 1971, *55,* 69-74.

Hogan, R. Pros and Cons of Performance-Based Teacher Training Program. *Proceedings—Conference on Involvement of the Liberal Arts in the New Texas Teacher Education Standards.* Austin, Texas: University of Texas at Austin, February 1973, 24.

Houston, W.R. Competency-Based Education. Chapter 1 in W.R. Houston,

*Exploring Competency-Based Education.* Berkeley, Calif.: McCutchan, 1974, 3-16.

Houston, W.R. *Strategies and Resources for Developing a Competency-Based Teacher Education Program.* Albany, N.Y.: New York State Education Department and Multi-State Consortium on Performance-Based Teacher Education, 1972.

Massanari, K. *CBTE and Professional Organizations.* Washington, D.C.: American Association of Colleges for Teacher Education, 1975.

McDonald, F. Unpublished paper of National Consortium for Performance Based Education. Princeton, N.J.: Educational Testing Service, 1974.

Merrow, J.G. *The Politics of Competency: A Review of Competency-Based Teacher Education.* Washington, D.C.: National Institute of Education, July 1974.

Morse, J.A. and M.H. Tellman. Effects on Achievement of Possession of Behavioral Objectives and Training Concerning Their Use. Paper presented at AERA Convention, Chicago, April 1972.

National Council on Education Professions Development. *Competency-Based Teacher Education: Toward a Consensus.* Washington, D.C.: NCEPD, Spring 1976.

Pittman, J. Actions Taken by State Departments of Education in Developing CBTE Certification Systems. A speech delivered at the ATE National Conference in New Orleans on February 6, 1975.

Rosner, B. and P. Kay. Will the Promise of Competency/Performance Based Teacher Education be Fulfilled? *Phi Delta Kappan,* 1974, *55,* 290-295.

Rothkopf, E.Z. and R. Kaplan. Exploration of the Effect of Density and Specificity of Instructional Objectives on Learning from Text. *Journal of Educational Psychology,* 1972, *63,* 295-302.

Schmieder, A.A. *Competency-Based Teacher Education: The State of the Scene.* Washington, D.C.: American Association of Colleges for Teacher Education, 1972.

Schmieder, A.A. The Last Relatively Complete Tentative Bibliography on Competency-Based Education. In W.R. Houston, *Exploring Competency-Based Education.* Berkeley, Calif.: McCutchan, 1974, 367-426.

Sherwin, S.S. *Performance-Based Teacher Education: Results of a Recent Survey.* Princeton: Educational Testing Service, 1974.

Soar, R. Accountability: Assessment Problems and Possibilities. *Journal of Teacher Education,* Fall 1973, *24,* 205-212.

Tarr, E.R. Some Philosophical Issues. In W.R. Houston, *Exploring Competency-Based Education.* Berkeley, Calif.: McCutchan, 1974, 79-90.

Westbrook, D.C. and W. Sandefur. Involvement of American Association of Colleges for Teacher Education Institutions in CBTE Programs. *Phi Delta Kappan,* December 1975, *57,* 276-277.

Wolk, S. The Influence of Meaningfulness Upon Intentional and Incidental Learning of Verbal Material. *Cognition,* 1973, *2,* 189-193.

# 8.
# Prospects for School Acceptance of Objectives-Based Instructional Progams

Fred C. Niedermeyer and
Howard J. Sullivan

The 1970s have seen a resolution of the controversy of the 1960s concerning the value of instructional objectives (e.g., Popham, Eisner, Sullivan and Tyler, 1969) and a general professional acceptance of their usefulness. Concurrently, there has been the emergence of a promising technology for development of comprehensive objectives-based instructional programs whose effectiveness has been verified through large-scale classroom tryouts. The development technology, which is primarily an outgrowth of federal support for programmatic instructional development efforts, involves a number of interrelated procedures (Niedermeyer, 1976; Sullivan, 1971) designed to ensure that an instructional program can consistently produce acceptable levels of pupil learning. These now-familiar procedures can be represented in abridged form as follows:

- Formulation of the instructional objectives for the program.
- Development of the instructional and implementation resources for the program and of the materials and procedures for assessing pupil attainment of each objective.
- Field testing of the program under the types of conditions in which it is intended to be used.
- Revision of program elements directly related to objectives which pupils do not successfully attain during field testing.
- Additional field testing and revision cycles until a comprehensive sample of pupils and classes successfully attain the program objectives.

The resources for effective objectives-based programs include a number of important elements (Niedermeyer and Moncrief, 1975). The instructional materials and procedures provide each pupil with abundant and direct practice on the instructional objectives and with regular, constructive feedback. Frequent diagnostic exercises permit assessment of pupil attainment of each objective and indicate whether additional instruction is needed. Less frequent cumulative tests reflecting broader proficiency are included to provide data on pupil performance on a comprehensive set of instructional objectives. Such data are useful for making decisions about program effectiveness and for reporting performance at the pupil, class, school and district levels to appropriate audiences.

Implementation resources are the materials and procedures needed by teachers and administrators to produce consistently successful results with the program. Included among these resources are (1) a list of the events to be completed by teachers, school-level administrators and district-level administrators in installation and use of the program, and (2) the materials for each event. Well-developed implementation resources also contain a system for routinely generating assessment-based reports to teachers, administrators and other audiences. These reports provide data at each desired level (pupil, class, school, district) on pupil attainment of program objectives and on the amount of the program completed. Procedures and materials may also be provided to assist school personnel in using the reports for such purposes as crediting instructional accomplishments or providing feedback designed to help individual teachers obtain better results. An additional essential item for an implementation or program-information guide is data on pupil performance during large-scale field testing of the program. Such data enable potential users to judge program effectiveness and to distinguish classroom-verified programs from the disturbing number of counterfeit objectives-based programs on which little or no user experience data have been collected.

The potential effectiveness of well-developed objectives-based programs is evident from Hanson and Schutz's (1975, 1976) reports of the evaluation of the SWRL Beginning Reading Program. Nationwide evaluation of this objectives-based program over a two-year period with more than 200,000 pupils representing the full range of socioeconomic and ethnic groups revealed that all groups attained high performance levels on the program objectives. When achievement differences were obtained between pupils on the basis of ethnic or socioeconomic background, the determinants of the achievement differences were not the demographic characteristics of the pupils. Instead, the differences were associated with a condition totally under the control of the schools—the amount of instructional time spent on the program. For example, when low-income or ethnic minority pupils received the same amount of instruction as middle-income or non-minority counterparts, they performed just as well on the program objectives.

Hanson and Schutz (1976) provide an encouraging interpretation of the implications of their data:

> These findings are important because they depart distinctly from contemporary conclusions regarding the effects of schooling. We refer here specifically to the popular "Coleman Report" . . . and the "Jencks Study" . . . . In both of these inquiries the effect of schooling was measured on norm-referenced achievement tests. The composite picture was that the effect of schooling is minimal relative to other factors such as the pupil's background, social status and "luck." That is, individual factors outside of control of the school were viewed as the prime determinants of achievement (pp. 1-2).

The outlook for development of objectives-based programs that can result in improved school achievement is promising. Results similar to the Hanson and Schutz data have been reported at the primary-grade level in language arts (reading, composition, and oral language) by Hanson, Behr, and Bailey (1975) and in nutrition education by Niedermeyer and Moncrief (1975). Large-scale efforts, centered mostly at educational research and development laboratories, are underway to develop objectives-based instructional programs in every major subject-matter area commonly included in the elementary schools.

Despite the promising outlook for development of effective objectives-based programs, the prospect for rapid adoption and implementation of such programs in the schools is not nearly so favorable. Publishers engaged in marketing efforts with well-developed objectives-based programs are experiencing difficulty. It appears that several common characteristics of such programs (e.g., abundant pupil practice, frequent assessment, designated teacher and administrator responsibilities, a system for reporting instructional accomplishments at various levels within a district) require difficult adjustments in thought and behavior by teachers and administrators. Just as educators voiced strong opposition to instructional objectives during the 1960s, many are now raising objections to objectives-based instructional programs.

Most of the concerns educators express about objectives-based programs appear to stem from misunderstandings or misinformation as to just what these programs are and are not. Generally, the concerns are without strong logical or operational bases; yet they are impediments to the acceptance and use of the programs. It seems important, therefore, to respond to these concerns, much as Popham (1967) responded some ten years ago to arguments against the use of instructional objectives. Several of the more popular and important concerns are listed below, followed by clarification or explanation designed to remove the concern as an obstacle to students and teachers receiving the benefits of the use of well-developed, objectives-based instructional programs.

### 1. We already have our own objectives.

Educator acceptance of the concept of instructional objectives has brought a multitude of efforts at local development of instructional objectives, mostly at the school district level. In some situations, each teacher is expected to develop his or her own objectives as a part of regular teaching duties. In others, committees are paid and/or given released time to develop a single set of objectives and a related assessment system. Often, the formulators of such efforts intend to collect data at some future time that indicates pupil performance levels on the objectives, though currently there are few local units where such data are being systematically collected.

Unfortunately, use of teacher- or committee-developed sets of objectives alone has little potential for yielding major improvements in pupil achievement related to the objectives. A number of research studies indicate that teachers are not successful at producing pupil accomplishment of instructional objectives when using traditional non-objectives-based instructional materials. For example, Baker (1968) found no difference between the posttest performance of pupils whose teachers were provided with precise behavioral objectives and those whose teachers used general non-behavioral objectives with the same instructional materials. A series of investigations by Popham (1971) indicated that experienced teachers serving as instructors produced no more learning in small groups of pupils than did housewives or other non-credentialed persons when each instructor was given a set of objectives plus resource materials and suggested learning activities. Similarly, Melaragno and Newmark (1968) found that kindergarten pupils demonstrated little or no more competency after instruction on objectives related to basic instructional concepts than on a pretest prior to teachers receiving the objectives and agreeing to "teach" them.

Neither providing teachers with a set of instructional objectives nor adding test items referenced to the objectives is likely to produce a high level of pupil attainment of the objectives. To successfully teach for pupil mastery of objectives, teachers must be provided with instructional materials and procedures developed especially for those objectives. Otherwise, they can be expected to do little else except to go on using the materials they have been using, whether these materials match the objectives or not. Merely providing the teachers with sets of objectives alone is likely to have little positive or negative effect, much like the age-old practice of providing curriculum guides or district goals. Serious injustice, however, is rendered by the increasingly popular practice of assessing pupil performance on the objectives and holding teachers accountable for specific performance levels when appropriate objectives-referenced resources are not made available. Without such resources, teachers should not be expected to accept accountability for high levels of pupil performance on the objectives.

*2. We are going to develop our
   own instructional materials.*

Development of instructional materials and procedures that teachers can use to consistently produce high levels of pupil achievement requires extensive amounts of time, money and expertise. A development project staff must include one or more persons with expertise in the subject-matter field of the program, objectives-based instructional development, applied human learning, and program evaluation, to name but a few areas. Several cycles of year-long tryout and revision of an instructional program are normally required before the program consistently yields acceptable results across large numbers of teachers. A highly experienced and specialized project staff in an educational research and development agency will typically spend several years developing an effective instructional program that spans a number of grades in a single subject. School districts are rarely, if ever, able to marshal and assign to a single project for an extended time period the resources and specialized expertise required for a successful major instructional development effort.

*3. Objectives-based instruction differs
   little from traditional instruction.*

Teachers using objectives-based programs for the first time sometimes remark that certain instructional activities seem to be time consuming or repetitious. They are accustomed to the "content-coverage" mode of traditional instruction in which they "cover" activities or pages of text with pupils, exposing them to information and content. The inappropriate teaching habits that can be developed in a content-coverage mode are illustrated by an observation study of 20 teachers conducting instruction during development of an objectives-based kindergarten reading program (Niedermeyer, 1970). It was found that teachers (1) asked for pupil responses that were appropriate to the objectives only one-third of the time, (2) elicited only one response every 15 seconds during group flashcard instruction, (3) never called on 40 percent of the pupils to make an individual response, (4) indicated correct responses only half of the time, (5) made a praising statement to pupils only once every six minutes, and (6) handled incorrect response in such ways that pupils rarely followed up with a correct response.

These actions are not surprising. Until recently, there has been little emphasis on clearly defining instructional objectives and developing pupils' proficiency on these objectives. The idea of taking the time required to provide pupils with the amounts of practice, feedback, and self-correction needed to acquire competency on objectives is still novel to many teachers. Therefore, abundant pupil practice and guidelines for effective teaching procedures are built directly into objectives-based programs—to assist teachers in successfully promoting pupil attainment of the objectives.

### 4. Objectives-based programs stifle teachers' creativity.

Some educators think of objectives-based instructional programs as "teacher-proof" products that turn the teacher into a robot-like programmed delivery system. Yet, that is not at all the case. Not only must objectives-based programs *not* be so regarded, they cannot in anyway be so used.

In a well-played version of the game of objectives-based instruction, teachers have the initial option of accepting or rejecting a program on the basis of their judgment of the worth of its objectives and resources for their pupils. If they decide to use the program, they agree to assess pupils periodically during the course of instruction to determine the degree to which the pupils have attained the objectives. There is no explicit requirement that teachers use all of the materials provided with the program or closely follow the recommended instructional procedures. The intention of the teachers and the program resources is to produce successful pupil performance on the objectives. To reach this goal teachers should and do use whatever effective resources and creative abilities they have.

The fact is that most teachers are happy to use the instructional materials in a well-developed objectives-based program, once they have tried them. The materials have previously been extensively tested in classrooms and revised for increased effectiveness and ease of use on the basis of teacher suggestions. Consequently, teachers find that such resources often save them preparation time and do not prevent them in any way from capitalizing on their particular instructional talents.

### 5. We don't use single programs because we match programs to individual learning styles.

Teachers are often advised to select two or more alternative instructional programs for the same set of instructional objectives or the same body of content. It is assumed that one program will be more effective for pupils with one unique "learning style" or set of characteristics and that other programs will be more effective for pupils with other characteristics.

The popularity of this "aptitude-treatment-interaction" notion has been far greater than its success as a guide for selecting or developing effective instructional resources. In general, the few well-planned research and development efforts aimed at improving achievement by matching pupil characteristics with existing materials or by developing special materials appropriate to particular pupil characteristics have not been successful (e.g., Baker, Schutz and Sullivan, 1971). There simply is no research evidence at this date that predictable aptitude-treatment-inter-actions exist to such a degree that they can be used successfully to match pupils with different instructional programs covering essentially the same content.

One characteristic on which it is particularly important to individualize instruction within a single program is each pupil's level of performance on the instructional objectives of the program. The frequent diagnostic exercises in a well-developed objectives-based program enable the teacher to readily identify pupils who have not yet attained given objectives and to differentiate instruction accordingly (Bloom, 1976).

### 6. Much of the testing in objectives-based programs is unnecessary.

Objectives-based instructional programs spanning several grades normally include at least three types of tests, all of which are keyed to the program objectives: a placement test indicating the level at which pupils should enter instruction, diagnostic tests for use on a regular basis (typically every few weeks) to assess pupil performance on a limited set of objectives, and comprehensive tests administered on approximately a once-a-semester or a once-a-year basis. Many teachers, particularly at the lower grade levels, object to the idea of regular testing and believe that their private judgments are the only necessary basis for making decisions about the initial placement of pupils in programs and their proficiency on instructional objectives.

Accurate initial placement of pupils in a program is very important. The aforementioned Hanson and Schutz study (1976) reports that kindergarten teachers typically did not place pupils at the level at which the reading placement test indicated they should enter the program. Most pupils were placed below the level indicated by the test, with ethnic minority and low-income pupils being placed far below the indicated level and much lower than other pupils relative to their placement test performance. These data suggest that teachers may hold unrealistically low expectations for such pupils that are detrimental to achievement. Such underplaced students do not, of course, progress as well as they could if they had not spent considerable amounts of time receiving instruction on objectives on which they were already proficient.

The diagnostic and comprehensive tests in an objectives-based program are designed primarily to indicate each pupil's performance on a set of objectives after pupils have received instruction on the objectives. Diagnostic testing in a well-developed program is simple and frequent enough to enable teachers to regularly identify and remediate instances of low achievement without the burdens of an onerous record-keeping system. Teachers using objectives-based programs do hear and/or observe many responses from individual pupils, and they undoubtedly are often able to make accurate judgments about the proficiency of their pupils on given objectives. The diagnostic tests simply provide a systematic basis for them to assess and record the performance of pupils on each objective, so that they can identify pupils who have attained the objectives and those who are still in need of additional instruction.

### 7. Objectives-based programs mean accountability.

The responsibility of the schools to produce acceptable levels of pupil achievement and to clearly communicate what is being learned in quantitative terms has received considerable attention during the past decade. Professional accountability is a complicated matter, and the schools have been understandably cautious in coming to accept it. Norm-referenced standardized tests are not highly sensitive to instructional treatments in the schools, and half of the pupils who take them must score below the mean for their reference group. Thus, it is inherently impossible for approximately half of the nation's schools to demonstrate instructional accomplishments in creditable ways when norm-referenced tests are used. Similarly, the use of objectives-referenced tests to measure pupil achievement in the traditional non-objectives-based programs currently being used in most schools is highly likely to yield data that are not at all favorable to the schools.

The use of well-developed objectives-based programs removes much of the risk of accountability because such programs provide a healthy basis for making instructional accomplishments visible and for demonstrating them to appropriate audiences. All of the necessary resources for assessing and reporting pupil performance are built directly into the program by its developers. With classroom-verified programs and objectives-referenced assessment, the probability is high that pupil performance levels will in fact be satisfactory and that schools can therefore receive appropriate credits for their successes (Moncrief, 1976). In cases where the performance of the program resources does not work as success-fully as expected, a well-developed program will contain materials and procedures for attempting to improve the less-than-satisfactory performance in a constructive manner.

The Program Report Service of the SWRL Communications Skills Programs (K-3 programs in reading, spelling, composition, and expressive language) is an example of an information system that can be used to regularly provide program-related data that are useful to the schools. The service generates monthly reports at three levels. Class reports, which are for use by the teacher, list performance by objective and program completion status for each pupil. School reports summarize pupil data by class and are most useful for the principal or other school-level officials in keeping informed of program performance by class and in crediting the accomplishments of teachers. District reports summarize the data by school and are intended for use by district administrators in crediting individual schools and publicizing district accomplish-ments with such groups as the school board, the community, and appropriate funding agencies. The service can also generate reports for parents of individual pupils. The entire service operates currently at a per-pupil total of less than one dollar a year for all four programs.

Classroom-verified objectives-based programs have the potential for enabling teachers to provide highly effective instruction. However, the realization of the benefits of such programs is severely limited if they include only instructional resources for use in the classroom. Without a reporting system for crediting instructional accomplishments and for noting and optimizing pupil progress, one can expect wide variability among teachers in the degree of classroom use of any given program and correspondingly wide variability among their classes with respect to achieving the objectives. A reporting system used in conjunction with associated implementation resources facilitates the cooperative efforts between teachers and administrators that are necessary for maximizing pupil progress and achievements throughout a school and district.

### 8. Instructional accountability is exclusively the responsibility of teachers.

Successful installation and operation of an instructional program is the joint responsibility of teachers, school-level administrators and district-level administrators. Too often, the schools merely supply instructional programs or materials for teachers and leave all further responsibility for successful instruction to them. Yet, professional responsibility for instructional success should not be placed solely upon teachers. If instances of unsatisfactory class performance are first detected by administrators at mid-year or the end of a year, then the administrators were not carrying out their responsibility of working cooperatively with teachers in identifying and overcoming such instances. Teachers should not accept the notion of instructional accountability if it is treated as their exclusive responsibility and is not properly shared throughout all levels of the district (Niedermeyer, 1976).

What can be done when program data indicate less-than-satisfactory progress or performance for particular classes or schools? A recent study (Niedermeyer, 1976) involving a kit of implementation resources for principals whose teachers were using an objectives-based reading program provides an example. Principals using the implementation resources worked with their teachers to (1) establish a reporting system, (2) set performance goals for rate of program completion and achievement of program objectives, (3) identify instances of class performance not meeting the agreed-upon goals, and (4) use suggestions and materials from the program to identify possible causes of low performance and to hypothesize and test instructional modifications designed to improve performances not meeting the goals. Pupils in the 24 schools using the implementation resources averaged 20 to 25 percent higher on program completion and performance on instructional objectives during the school year than did pupils in 12 comparable schools using the objectives-based reading program without the implementation resources.

Objectives-referenced supervision differs markedly from traditional means-oriented supervision in which such factors as teaching technique, class control, and classroom and personal appearance receive heavy emphasis (McNeil, 1966; Smithman and Lucio, 1974). With the proper resources for objectives-referenced supervision, school administrators have the opportunity for effective instructional leadership that is goal-oriented and will be supported by teachers. They will spend their supervisory time crediting teachers for their instructional accomplishments and working cooperatively with them to bring about improvements in performance when such improvements are clearly needed.

## Looking Ahead

Large-scale objectives-based instructional development is a young field, emerging primarily from modest federal support for programmatic instructional research and development beginning in the late 1960s. What about the future? As the number of well-developed objectives-based programs increases, will educators continue to raise objections to their use? Or will the initial concerns be replaced by a greater willingness to accept and use such programs, such as the arguments against instructional objectives that were so common only a few years ago have now been replaced by a general acceptance of such objectives?

The answers to the above questions will be influenced both by the response of the schools to the increasing pressures for demonstrating tangible outcomes of schooling and by the ability of educational organizations developing objectives-based programs to help schools meet this challenge. As the number of comprehensive objectives-based programs increases, their use in the schools is bound to increase also. Educational development organizations must supply convincing evidence of the consistent effectiveness of their objectives-based programs and they must provide schools with the means to do likewise. If such evidence is regularly obtained in the schools and used to credit school accomplishments, then the future is promising for the acceptance and implementation of objectives-based programs.

# References

Baker, E.L. *The Differential Effect of Giving Behavioral and Non-behavioral Objectives to Teachers on the Achievements of Their Students.* Paper presented at annual meeting of the California Educational Research Association, Berkeley, California, 1968.

Baker, R.L., R.E. Schutz and H.J. Sullivan. An Application of Guilford's Structure of Intellect to Programmed Instruction. In R.A. Weisgerber (Ed.), *Perspectives in Individualized Learning.* Itasca, Ill.: F.E. Peacock, 1971, 79-97.

Bloom, B.S. *Human Characteristics and School Learning.* New York: McGraw-Hill, 1976.

Hanson, R., G. Behr and J. Bailey. *SWRL Communication Skills Programs: Quality Assurance Information for the 1973-74 Academic Year.* Technical Report 54, SWRL Educational Research and Development, Los Alamitos, California, 1975.

Hanson, R. and R. Schutz. *The Effects of Programmatic R&D on Schooling and the Effects of Schooling on Students.* Technical Report 53, SWRL Educational Research and Development, Los Alamitos, California, 1975.

Hanson, R. and R. Schutz. *Instructional Product Implementation and Schooling Effects.* SWRL Technical Report 56, SWRL Educational Research and Development, Los Alamitos, California, 1976.

McNeil, J. Antidote to a School Scandal. *Educational Forum*, November 1966, *31*, 69-77.

Melaragno, R. and J. Newmark. *A Pilot Study to Apply Evaluation-Revision*

*Procedures in First-Grade Mexican-American Classrooms: Final Report.*
System Development Corporation, Santa Monica, California, 1968.

Moncrief, M. *The Use of Instructional Management Information Systems in
Crediting the Schools' Instructional Accomplishments.* SWRL Educational
Research and Development, Los Alamitos, California, 1976.

Niedermeyer, F. *Developing Exportable Teacher Training for Criterion-Referenced Instructional Programs.* Technical Report 22, SWRL Educational
Research and Development, Los Alamitos, California, 1970.

Niedermeyer, F. and M. Moncrief. Primary-Graders Study Nutrition. *Elementary School Journal,* February 1975, *75,* 304-310.

Niedermeyer, F. Developing Classroom-Based Instructional Products: An
Evolving Set of Guidelines. *Educational Technology,* November 1976,
55-57.

Niedermeyer, F. A Basis for Improved Instructional Leadership. *The
Elementary School Journal,* January 1977, 248-254.

Niedermeyer, F. The Testing of a Prototype System for Outcomes-Based
Instructional Supervision. *Educational Administration Quarterly,* Spring
1977, 34-50.

Popham, W.J. *Probing the Validity of Arguments Against Behavioral
Objectives.* Paper presented at Annual Conference of California Advisory
Council on Educational Research, San Diego, 1967.

Popham, W.J., E.W. Eisner, H.J. Sullivan and L.L. Tyler. *Instructional
Objectives.* AERA Curriculum Monograph No. 3. Chicago: Rand McNally,
1969.

Popham, W.J. Performance Tests of Teaching Proficiency: Rationale, Development and Validation. *American Educational Research Journal,* January
1971, *8,* 105-117.

Smithman, H. and W. Lucio. Supervision by Objectives: Pupil Achievement as
a Measure of Teacher Performance. *Educational Leadership,* January 1974,
*31,* 338-344.

Sullivan, H. Developing Effective Objectives-Based Instruction. *Educational
Technology,* July 1971, *11,* 55-57.

# 9.
# A Synergistic View
# of Behavioral Objectives
# and Behavior Modification

Terrence Piper

Many professionals in the field of education assume an intimate relationship between writing behavioral objectives and practicing the principles of behavior modification. In fact, there is very little necessary relationship. While the two competency sets are readily compatible, a teacher, for example, may be highly skilled in writing and sequencing curriculum objectives and yet may be unfamiliar with the most fundamental principles of behavior modification. Similarly, a school psychologist may consult with teachers daily on the organizing of behavior modification programs in response to behavior problems but may be unable to compose a single simple objective in reading. A given professional may excel in both areas of competency, in either area or in neither. Definition of the parameters of each set of competencies referred to above should promote a better understanding of differences and commonalities between the two and may promote unique and desirable blends.

## Behavioral Objectives and
## Curriculum Programming

Until a child, in some way, demonstrates the acquisition of a given skill or knowledge, the teacher cannot know that the child has learned. In composing a behavioral objective, the teacher merely indicates what it is that the child must do to communicate that he has learned (the behavior), how well he must do it (the criteria) and under what circumstances (the conditions). It is necessary to indicate relevant conditions as these may make the behavior more or less easy to perform. An objective is complete when all three considerations—behavior, criteria, and conditions—are identified (Mager, 1962). Writing objectives, then, involves the skills of identifying what is to be learned and when it has been satisfactorily learned. Since it is the teacher's job to teach and to assess learning, these skills are highly desirable.

An objective becomes far more useful when placed into a series of related objectives. That is, the teacher should identify not only what the child needs to do to demonstrate that he has achieved the current objective, but also what the child needs to know and demonstrate *before* attempting the current objective, and what he will attempt to learn *after* mastering the current objective. A series of related objectives, placed in appropriate order, is synonymous with a well-defined curriculum. Curriculum programming is identifying the parts of a curriculum in the order in which the parts will best be taught. The prescriptive teaching process and individualization of instruction necessitates the placement of each child along a sequential series of objectives. Similarly, group instruction for skill acquisition requires the placement of a group along a series of objectives. Anyone (teacher, administrator, parent or the child himself) who has reason to be interested in the progress of a child or group of children, and in the documentation of that progress, has reason to be interested in behavioral objectives and the sequencing of objectives.

### Behavior Modification

The terms "behavior modification" or, more specifically, "operant conditioning," refer here to that body of knowledge and competencies with which the teacher structures the environment so that the consequences of a given behavior affect that behavior in a desirable direction. That is, behaviors that are appropriate for the classroom are increased or maintained while those that are inappropriate are decreased. The fundamental assumption underlying behavior modification is that we do what we do in order to minimize those events or stimuli that we, as individuals, find to be aversive (O'Leary and O'Leary, 1972). Rewards can be objectively defined, even for the most disturbed individual, as stimuli that maintain or increase the behavior that precedes them. The stimulus that reduces the preceding behavior is designated aversive. Furthermore, consequences that closely follow a behavior are more effective than consequences that are delayed.

While the brief explanation of behavior modification given above is an oversimplification, nevertheless certain basic applied principles follow. The child who behaves well or makes a correct response should, as a consequence, be rewarded. Or, if an aversive stimulus is already on-going or threatened, the aversive stimulus or the threat should be reduced. The former procedure is referred to as positive reinforcement while the latter is negative reinforcement. If the teacher can assume that a child misbehaves or makes errors in order to get a reward (such as attention) for the behavior in the past, then the teacher should avoid the presentation of the reward after misbehavior, a procedure called extinction. Similarly, the teacher should increase the probability of rewards when the child does not misbehave, a procedure called differential reinforcement of other behavior (DRO). If the child behaves inappropriately in a preferred environment, he may be temporarily removed (time out) to a less preferred environment. Fines (response cost) or the introduction of any aversive stimulus (punishment) also serves to reduce undesirable behavior. Whatever the choice, the consequence will be more effective if it quickly follows the behavior. While these techniques may appear to be a statement of common sense, as they are, systematic application of these techniques may often become very complex. This is especially true in the case of complicated token systems and contracts, or in the identification of rewards for disturbed, severely handicapped, and socially atypical individuals. Multiple consequences, such as the simultaneous giving of rewards by peers and punishment by the teacher, may also have conflicting effects. The varying probabilities of certain consequences and often unusual schedules of reinforcement may further complicate what may at first have seemed simple (Piper, 1974a).

### Operational Commonalities

Up to this point, the differences between the two sets of competencies have been stressed. Yet, at least two relationships that constitute commonalities must exist.

Informally, every teacher engages in the basics of curriculum programming as well as behavior modification, since both are necessary aspects of any instructional program. While necessity itself may be a shared characteristic, it is the operational commonalities that are likely to cause professionals to confuse the two. These appear only when the two competency areas are formally applied.

In the first place, *both curriculum programming and behavior modification require operational or behavioral definitions of the behavior that is of concern.* To say that "Johnny lacks respect for others," is too vague for either a behavioral objective or the conceptualization of a behavior modification strategy. The concern for Johnny's social development must first be operationalized. For example, Johnny calls both peers and adults certain foul or derogatory names which might then be listed. The operationalization of behavior, as a common initial step, may account for many instances of confusion.

Secondly, *both curriculum programming and behavior modification assume that efficient learning depends on appropriate feedback.* This second commonality occurs most noticeably when curriculum programming is highly formalized, as in the case of programmed instruction for teaching machines of all sorts. All teaching machines rely upon knowledge of results for positive reinforcement of correct responses. The learner is rewarded, in one way or another, by being told he made a correct response and instructed to move on to the next frame. Should he err, the error is ignored, as in extinction, and the original frame is usually presented again. More sophisticated machines add greater amounts of positive reinforcement to knowledge of results, as in the case of point counters or token dispensers.

Programmed instruction is a useful example of the integration into one teaching procedure of the two sets of competencies involved in curriculum programming and behavior modification. First the teacher presents material to the child to provide stimulus cues and information that will allow the child to make the correct response. The teacher is responsible for presenting the materials, or "antecedents." Secondly, the child makes some sort of response to the material—verbal, written or other physical movement or behavior. Third, the teacher responds to the child's response so as to let him know that he is right or wrong and so as to motivate appropriate performance in the future. The third part of teaching is referred to as the "consequence." Notice that the teacher is responsible for structuring both the antecedents and the consequences in order to stimulate and maintain appropriate or correct behavior from the child. The antecedents are primarily, for academic behaviors at least, curriculum programming. The consequences are behavior modification. The teacher structures the classroom environment, both antecedents and consequences, in order to maximally promote learning.

## The Past

Until the last decade, teachers structured learning environments largely on the basis of personal preference and experience. Teacher training was all too often unrelated to the applied setting. Teaching was truly an art wherein some were good and some were not so good, and very few observers were prepared to say why in either case. Therefore, historically teachers have been promoted on the basis of seniority, the one objective criterion in the entire field. Supervisory help and inservice training often helped teachers improve, but that help was nearly always situation specific rather than being based on a given set of guiding principles. University training focused almost entirely on antecedents, as in the classic curriculum and methods courses. New teachers were worried most about controlling student behavior because they were so ill-prepared to solve problems in behavior management. In any case, most pupils learned anyway. In instances where they did not, the fault was assumed to lie within the child, and he was labeled "retarded" or "disturbed." Behavioral objectives could be found in textbooks, tests, worksheets and in the teacher's mind, but they were disguised and informal. Behavior management was similarly disguised, and it depended on luck and the teacher's personality. Social reinforcement was widely used but often in negative ways. Symbolic reinforcers such as grades, smiling faces, honor roles and athletic trophies also were used, but with lengthy delays in reinforcement so as to reduce their overall effectiveness and to limit their effectiveness to older and brighter children. Material reinforcers were referred to as "bribes," especially when these were primary reinforcers (even though linguistically the term "bribe" should refer primarily to reinforcement of illegal or inappropriate behavior). The "bribery reaction" was probably in response to applications of positive reinforcement procedures using reinforcers that were unnecessarily large or unnecessarily primary in nature for children that were clearly capable of responding to more abstract, secondary reinforcers. Teachers were quick to imagine that if Johnny is given a candy bar for completing his work, he might regress to doing his work *only* if given similar primary reinforcers. Reviews of early classroom application (e.g., Axelrod, 1971) find many researchers over-reinforcing or using reinforcers generally considered inappropriate by most teachers and school administrators. Perhaps generalizations from the laboratories of the 1940s and 50s to classrooms of the 60s were too direct. Thus, the researcher, in his zeal for significant results, may have unwittingly delayed common realization of the everyday value of formalized reinforcement techniques.

**The Present**
While the misunderstandings of past years are becoming

clarified, there is a simultaneous growth in the sophistication and application of behavioral techniques. Publishers of textbook series now commonly identify objectives, either separately or within the texts themselves. These vary widely, of course, in terms of quality (Ohrtman, 1976). For example, a simplistic statement of behavior may be presented without regard either to performance criteria or to performance circumstances. More sophisticated textbook series are usually careful to identify circumstances, but may intentionally avoid criteria specifications so that these might vary with teacher preference and the differing needs of children. Nearly all current publications, however, avoid making vague, unmeasurable definitions of behavior. The well-trained teacher is now given enough information to formulate complete and useable objectives for nearly all of the widely used textbook series. Some of the most updated series, for example the Heath Elementary Mathematics series (Dilley *et al.*, 1975), provide the teacher with exceptionally complete and carefully sequenced objectives. Such series also suggest the methodology and materials needed to individualize instruction and to evaluate progress with relative ease.

Clear and well-sequenced objectives are necessary for both the diagnostic-prescriptive teaching process and the individualization of instruction. The teacher identifies where the child is academically at any given moment and specifies what is to be taught next. Frequent re-evaluation is necessary in order to continue to move the child along the behavioral sequence as he learns. In special education, and to a lesser extent in the entire field of education, progress can now be systematically charted. The recording system may be as simple as a checklist of objectives for each child or as complex as the log charting advocated by Lindsley (1970) in what he describes as "precision teaching."

A foundation for a self-improving educational technology is developing, perhaps leading to the most dramatic and exciting period in the history of education. The careful and frequent recording of progress not only facilitates the quality and accuracy of individualized instruction, but it also allows for the evaluation

and continued improvement of teaching techniques. Ineffective
methods, for children in general or for an exceptional child,
should be easily identifiable so that others can be tried. Thus,
these developments, with all their obvious promise for the quality
of education for children, also facilitate teacher evaluation and
accountability. Some teachers, for this reason, become uncomfort-
able when asked to document child progress, and have sought
support from teacher unions. Conflict, in a period of change and
development, should be expected. The courts, apparently antici-
pating the resistance, have already acted to promote the interests
of the child. In addition, Public Law 94-142, passed by the 94th
Congress on November 29, 1975, and designed for complete
implementation by October 1, 1977, requires that there be an
annual evaluation for every child placed in a special education
program. In the case of reports relating to performance, information is to be provided that is .in accordance with specific
performance criteria related to program objectives (section 614,
part 3-A). Therefore, at least for special education programs,
school districts must develop objectives, including criteria, and
must evaluate children in regard to the objectives met before,
during, and after special intervention. The consequence for not
following this pattern is specified in the law as the loss of all
federal funds for the delinquent district.

Contingency management also has progressed from the "M &
M" stereotype to methodology far more palatable to most
educators. Research regarding the potency of social reinforcement
in the classroom dates back to the mid 1960s (Becker *et al.*,
1967). As this research regarding the effects of common reinforcers came to be digested by teachers, supervisors and teacher
trainers, it became increasingly clear that all teachers use behavior
modification principles, whether or not they know that they are
doing so. The professional responsibility for knowing *what* one is
doing and *why* one does it has forced many minds, long closed to
M & Ms, to reconsider the subject.

Other common classroom reinforcers, including teacher proximity, grades, stickers, classroom jobs, time to work on projects, free time, and the like, have been recognized as effective (Piper, 1974b). The effects of schedules of reinforcement as well as delays of reinforcement are consciously considered in many classrooms for added efficiency and effect. Nearly all teacher training programs offered today require some sort of training in, or at least exposure to, behavior modification. In this author's view, the professionals best trained to apply learning theory to pragmatic classroom situations graduate increasingly from education departments rather than from psychology departments.

## The Future

The field of education has advanced technologically at an ever increasing rate. There are now more methods than ever, documented to be effective, available to teach both the learner who is eager and the learner who is not. An obvious speculative prediction would be one of continued growth in the field of education until it is more true science than art. If one acknowledges education's function as the indoctrination and training of the young for a place in society, adding strength to do so may prove to be more frightening than beneficial. Who is to decide who is to be trained to do what? Perhaps we are advancing toward the "brave new world" described by Aldous Huxley. While we may not, as educators, control the domain of fetal environments, we are learning more about how best to control educational (and potentially indoctrinational) environments after birth in order to make sure our curricula are learned.

Simultaneously, there are many children in schools today who are not learning to read and who will not know basic arithmetic well enough to calculate their own income tax. Any change that increases the effectiveness of educational programs is needed by these children and will ultimately add freedom to their adult lives.

Concern for the power of education wanes in the light of so many failures. The field is so large and inconsistent in both practice and philosophy that knowledge is rarely utilized to its fullest potential. No consciencious educator would suggest that we not teach tool subjects or self-help skills, or that the ability to use language to maximize communication skills is not a desirable asset for any child. It would seem probable, then, that the technological advances related to behavior modification or the use of behavioral objectives will be most acceptable for teaching "tool subjects" and communication skills.

Trends for the future are already a reality in some of the most advanced programs of today. Rather than report grades to parents, the teacher might list objectives met during the last evaluation period. Token systems will be developed wherein tokens are earned for reaching objectives, rather than for appropriate social behavior. Promotions will not be based on numbers of years in attendance, but on objectives met. School systems will define curricula in sequences of objectives so that diplomas can indicate objectives met before graduation. Self-contained classrooms for mildly handicapped students will become rare or non-existent, while regular classrooms might be organized around teaching a particular span of objectives.

The use of formalized contingency management for academic behaviors will be seen as unfair and inappropriate for many children in the class unless instruction is individualized to an appreciable extent. For example, if the children are told that they can each receive a token for completion of the exercise on page 129, some children will have to work long and hard to complete the task while others will breeze through it with no effort. A more desirable procedure would be to offer the token for "task completion," with a variety of tasks matched to each child's level of achievement. Again, the use of contingency management and individualized instruction must progress simultaneously.

Charting procedures of various kinds (Piper, 1974b) will become commonplace. A major source of reinforcement will be charting progress toward meeting current objectives. The child will be rewarded by seeing himself progress. Meeting certain objectives will signal moving to another group or classroom, a very potent reinforcer. Schools will be better organized to promote the use of reinforcers that have educational value. For example, a large space might contain calculators and computer terminals for math work and research in one corner, chemistry lab equipment in another, art materials in another, and a small home economics set-up in another. Special projects with designated levels of difficulty, matched to certain classroom objectives, would be on file for each high-interest station. A paraprofessional might be assigned to facilitate or help when necessary. Children would earn the privilege of visiting the room, contingent upon meeting objectives. In similar ways, schools could re-design libraries, develop music rooms including popular, ethnic, folk and classical sections, develop student lounges, special project areas, and a program of field trips, speakers and movies, all of which would be designed to encourage children to meet objectives while at the same time broadening educational experiences. Lists of projects or activities that parents might be encouraged to develop at home could be correlated with mastery of specific objectives. The parent could be systematically involved in helping the child to generalize skills learned in school to environments outside the school. Classroom supplies and new textbooks also might be earned by making progress.

Teachers will be routinely observed and given objective feedback regarding their use of social reinforcement. For example, the rate of attending to appropriate behaviors will be calculated and compared to the rate of attending to inappropriate behaviors. Rapport and communication will be maintained at positive levels so that children will be more likely to relate well to teachers, schools, and school-type activities.

In summary, the future will see a more consistent and coordinated use of behavioral objectives and behavior modification, especially in regard to tool subjects and other curricula identified as necessary for all children. Reinforcement for reaching or approaching objective mastery will be commonplace and instruction will be necessarily more individualized. Less emphasis will be placed on managing social behaviors, because the child cannot work diligently toward meeting objective criteria and "goof-off" at the same time. Schools will expand the variety of reinforcers available to the teacher, especially those that complement and generalize the skills and knowledge referred to in given behavioral objectives.

Communication systems with parents will focus on *what each child has learned* rather than on general statements of achievement. Classes will be organized and grouped according to particular objectives. It would follow that mainstreaming of mildly handicapped students into classes on the basis of achievement will become a natural reality. The gifted student also will progress at his own rate until, when all tool subjects are mastered, he will be free to organize his own curriculum according to interest, needs and career goals.

## References

Axelrod, S. Token Reinforcement Programs in Special Classes. *Exceptional Children*, January 1971, *37*, 371-379.

Becker, W.C., C.H. Madsen, C.R. Arnold and D.R. Thomas. The Contingent Use of Teacher Attention and Praise in Reducing Classroom Behavior Problems. *The Journal of Special Education*, Spring 1967, *1*, 287-307.

Dilley, C., W. Rucker, A. Jackson, J.R. Dennis, G. Rising, M. Griffith and M. Bekerman. *Heath Elementary Mathematics.* Boston, Mass.: D.C. Heath and Co., 1975.

Lindsley, O. *Behavior Bank*. P.O. Box 3937, Kansas City, Kansas, BB, 1970.

Mager, R.F. *Preparing Instructional Objectives*. Belmont, Calif.: Fearon Publishers, 1962.

Ohrtman, W.S. (principal investigator). *Special Education Resources Location Analysis and Retrieval System* (SER-LARS). King of Prussia, Pa.: National Learning Resource Center of Pennsylvania, Federal Grant 300-75-0034, 1976.

O'Leary, K.D. and S.G. O'Leary. *Classroom Management*. Elmsford, N.Y.: Pergamon Press, 1972.

Piper, T. *Classroom Management and Behavioral Objectives: Applications of Behavior Modification*. Belmont, Calif.: Fearon Publishers, 1974a.

Piper, T. *Materials for Classroom Management: Catch 'Em Being Good*. Belmont, Calif.: Fearon Publishers, 1974b.

# 10.
# The Behavioral Objectives Movement: Its Impact on Physical Education

Anita J. Harrow

A few years ago, educators were introduced to a new concept called behavioral objectives. The wave of this new movement was at first small and created no great notice. Then suddenly it swelled and more educators began to recognize and become concerned with the inevitable changes in programs that could occur as a result of this new concept.

As with any new idea introduced into an existing traditional program, the behavioral objectives movement met with varied responses, both positive and negative, from professionals across the nation. Some educators hailed the movement as a boon to education and as a much needed revitalizing force. Others were concerned that the movement was a fluke and believed it would pass into oblivion with time. After more than a decade, behavioral objectives in perhaps a more sophisticated form are still very much on the educational scene. It is our task as educators to take the best from this experience and move ahead.

This chapter will focus on the behavioral objectives movement with respect to the discipline of physical education. When we discuss physical education as a discipline, we must deal with three major identifiable components, the academic, the professional and the functional. In addition, this chapter will explore the possibilities that emerged from the behavioral objectives movement for a renewed, competency-based, teaching-learning model for teacher education. This model will be specific to physical education but will be applicable to other disciplines. The model will suggest a possible program structure for the future.

### Three Components of Physical Education

All of the three specific components—academic, professional, functional—within physical education have been affected by the behavioral objectives movement. However, more of an impact has been made in the public school systems, where physical education focuses primarily on the functional component. Teacher education institutions have the major responsibility for educating qualified instructors for public school systems and thus the impact of the movement has been perhaps of equal if not greater concern to them.

The primary role of an educator in the academic component of physical education is that of scholar-researcher—one who makes inquiry into appropriate and related subject matter. A basic and continuing characteristic of the academic function is to investigate and understand a portion of the reality which is defined by the discipline. Thus, physical education as an academic discipline becomes a conceptual subject matter focused on the phenomenon of human movement.

In the professional component, the process rather than the content of physical education is emphasized. An attempt is made to foster student development through the flexible process of engaging in lifelike movement activities. This stems from the belief that education *is* life, not preparation *for* life. The primary role of an educator functioning in this component is that of a performer-teacher.

The functional component takes existing knowledge and applies it to the use of human movement in an effort to obtain certain developmental results. Students are helped to develop physical attributes which underlie all kinds of purposeful movement, to develop a personal "movement vocabulary," and to become effective and efficient in the art and science of human movement. The present definition of physical education includes "the art and science of human movement." Thus, physical education is a discipline which encompasses all facts, knowledge and understandings of human movement related to the fullest actualization of the individual within his environmental setting. It is time to look ahead to an ever improving physical education for a new and different world.

The functional component of physical education appears to be once again at the point of the pendulum swing, this time with the hope of total revitalization by way of commitment to a stronger philosophy and a more specific statement of values and goals. The behavioral objectives movement, though not the initiator, may have been the impetus for such change. The movement has perhaps given the field of physical education more visibility among educators in other disciplines. At one time not too long ago, the physical education program was considered by many educators to be a recreation program; some educators may still be guilty of his faulty perspective. However, more informed educators now recognize the values students gain from a comprehensive movement education program that spans kindergarten through adult leisure activities.

With the present status of the world, more people are realizing the value and role of movement activities. Research has indicated that movement is central to each individual in relating to others, in learning, in accepting oneself, in establishing self/life values, and in becoming an effective, productive human being.

## Behavioral Objectives and
## Physical Education

The physical educator is one of the few educators who has assumed the responsibility of being accountable for student development in all three domains of learning—the affective, cognitive and psychomotor. To design a comprehensive physical education program using behavioral objectives requires an educator who has an awareness of the content of the discipline, who is adept at curriculum design, and who can effectively incorporate the learning domains in a comprehensive program. Few teacher education institutions have developed competency-based programs in these particular areas. Thus, many professionals lack the specific competencies necessary to incorporate behavioral objectives representing all three learning domains into a curriculum.

Educators who have carefully analyzed what has actually occurred as a result of the behavioral objectives movement have ascertained many familiar and valuable teacher competencies emerging. For example, they have recognized that there is little new in this current movement; good teachers have always defined their educational goals, tried many different teaching techniques, and attempted to evaluate the learning that occurred. These educators saw the behavioral objectives movement for what it was—an attempt to communicate more specifically the goals of education in all curricular areas, a move toward educational accountability and, hopefully, an improved system of education for the youth of this country.

It appears that the concern over behavioral objectives has brought about a new awareness of the balance that is needed between the logical, systematic and controlled approach to education as defined by science, and the knowledge gained from branches of learning which center on human aspirations and ideals. In other words, there appears to be a new combining of the scientific and the humanistic—the critical and the creative. This cooperative effort brings educators together to work as a team, each having a significant responsibility in an area of specialization that is separate but directly related to other areas of knowledge. The goal of this cooperative effort is the harmonious development of the whole individual. In order to continue the progress forward, educators must take the significant values from the behavioral objectives movement and continue toward the ultimate goal of improved education for youth.

Now appears to be an opportune time for professionals in all components of physical education to come to the support of a unified philosophical statement encompassing the many goals of a total commitment to an improved physical education curriculum. It is through the use of the behavioral objectives approach that this can be accomplished. If critically viewed, the entire emphasis placed on educational accountability and behavioral objectives can lead toward a new model for teacher education, one with a common core of teacher competencies which include both basic skills and the art of teaching.

## A Teaching-Learning Model

Tyler's (n.d.) systematic approach to education and accountability encompasses clarity of purpose, allowance for student performance, accuracy of evaluation, and opportunity for reorganizing for enhanced student learning. His process model is as follows:

1. Identify specific educational goals and objectives.
2. Select a specific behavior in which students will be involved.
3. Provide a situation in which the behavior can occur.
4. Design and apply instruments for observing and/or recording outcomes of student involvement.
5. Determine from the evidence observed the implications for the next learning step.

The Tyler model can be used for all types of teaching-learning situations regardless of the learning domain into which the behavior falls.

By contrast, a humanistic approach to education provides a student with a learning environment which helps the student develop a sense of self worth and responsibility for those around him. Humanistic education encourages students to be self-directed learners who will take responsibility for and enjoy life-long learning. Students learn "how" to acquire knowledge, to develop physical abilities and to attain skill mastery. This instills in each student the courage to try new things rather than just repeating what others have done. It also stimulates the urge to be creative.

The teaching-learning model proposed here (Figure 1) is a balance between the scientific approach and the humanistic

*Figure 1*

*Teaching-Learning Model: Characteristics of an Effective Teacher*

Effective Teacher

1.1 Possesses Communication Skills

1.2 Understands Relevant Learning Theories

1.3 Understands Basic Instructional Techniques

1.4 Understands Basic Skills of Curriculum Design

1.5 Possesses Necessary Skills for Art of Teaching (Selection of Instructional Strategies)

Statement of Philosophy

Utilization of Goal Setting Process

Development of Behavioral Objectives Writing Skill

Utilization of Learning Domain

Analysis of Content Area

Utilization of Systems Analysis Approach

Understanding of Affective Development

Application of Mastery Learning Techniques

Application of Motivational Theory

Application of Learning Theory

Integration of Theory with Reality

approach. It is one in which both the art and science of education play equally important roles. Although all of the levels identified in Figure 1 are important, we will explore only levels 1.4 and 1.5, since this is where behavioral objectives begin to influence the teaching-learning model proposed here.

It should be noted that levels 1.4 and 1.5 incorporate Riles' (1971) emphasis on (1) definition of goals, (2) arrangement of resources, (3) design of evaluation, and (4) selection of a variety of appropriate instructional strategies.

*Level 1.4: Basic Skills of*
*Curriculum Design*

The model suggests that an effective educator must possess certain competencies which are necessary prerequisites to the basic skills of curriculum design. Inherent within the curriculum design category are the competencies of (1) acceptance of an educational philosophy, (2) identification of educational purpose, (3) selection of a behavioral objectives writing technique, (4) utilization of learning domains, (5) techniques of analyzing a content area, and (6) utilization of a systems analysis technique. Let us examine briefly each of these competencies.

*Philosophy*. First, an educator must select the philosophical approach which will best reflect his educational beliefs. The educator should choose between the idealist, the realist and the pragmatist approaches, or a combination of the three. The idealist believes the purpose of education to be the full development of each individual and the ultimate realization of an ideal society. The realist believes the purpose of education to be the attainment of verified knowledge to build competencies designed to help individuals understand and make adjustments to the real, external world. The nature of the curriculum under a realist approach would be a rigorous and systematically organized subject matter which emphasized transmission and mastery of scientific facts and principles. The pragmatist believes the purposes of education to be the successful solution of problems in everyday life and the development of socially acceptable and functional members of society. The nature of the curriculum under a pragmatic approach would focus on activities which would give the student experience in applying the scientific method to the solution of problems closely related to community and current situations. Emphasis in the physical education curriculum would be on cooperation, performing, and problem solving through sports and games.

The understanding of the variety of philosophical approaches under which a program can be designed, the selection of a particular philosophy, and the ability to communicate a professional philosophy to others constitutes an important competency educators should possess. A philosophy of an educational program could function as the basis for program goal selection.

*Goal setting.* The second component of "basic skills of curriculum design" is the statement of educational goals around which the curriculum will evolve. The behavioral objectives movement recognizes the essential role played by statements of specific educational goals which serve to define the purposes of education programs. Many authors have expounded on the necessity for stating goals. However, McAshan (1974) explains not only the value of goal statements, but the specific details of how to develop and use a "goals approach" writing technique in curriculum design.

The over-all educational purpose of a program, or "mission statement," could emerge from a variety of sources which include the stated philosophy of the program, professional judgment and observation, a comprehensive needs assessment, and guidelines from professional associations and/or state educational agencies. From the mission statement are derived the specific component goals of the program.

Since the statement of specific goals serves to define the purposes of the program and reflect the content to be covered, it seems logical to include the ability to specifically state educational goals as an important competency for educators. Without specifically stated goals, a program would lack clarity of purpose, direction, and comprehensiveness. It is at this point in curriculum design that content area expertise and comprehension of the three learning domains are essential.

*Behavioral objectives writing.* The third component of the basic skills of curriculum design is the writing of behavioral objectives. To possess competence in this area, an educator must have developed an understanding of evaluation theory and assessment techniques and must be aware of differences between norm-referenced and criterion-referenced measurement. In addition, the educator should know something about test construction and should develop basic abilities related to designing an over-all evaluation system to determine program accountability. It is important, however, that educators do not get caught up in the "bell curve" trap, thereby dooming some students to failure. Evaluation and assessment are just tools used by educators and students to determine areas of strengths upon which to build and weaknesses which must be remedied so that continuous successful learning can proceed. Knowledge of several different theories is prerequisite to competency in assessment. Probably one of the most enlightening theories is the mastery learning concept by Bloom *et al*. (1971). They state:

> Most students (perhaps over 90 percent) can master what we have to teach them, and it is the task of instruction to find the means which will enable our students to master the subject under consideration. Our basic task is to determine what we mean by mastery of the subject and to search for the methods and materials which will enable the largest proportion of our students to attain such mastery (p. 43).

The development of a curriculum stated in terms of behavioral objectives goes hand in hand with the mastery learning concept and criterion-referenced evaluation. This particular competency of behavioral objectives writing is, in the author's opinion, the foundation of curriculum design. An educator should understand the force behind the behavioral objectives movement, the difference between the two major writing techniques (goals approach and outcomes approach) and the procedure for incorporating behavioral objectives writing techniques into the teacher education curriculum.

Not only must the theory and technique of evaluation be understood, but also the procedure for product and process evaluation of movement activities must be mastered. Physical educators continuously conduct product evaluation, which involves the measurement of quality of the movement. This appears as a summary score, such as how many, how far, how high, how fast. Process evaluation, which involves characteristics of the movement task, is more difficult to conduct. Process evaluation provides a description of how a student uses his body to accomplish a movement task; process analysis provides information relative to a student's level of development in a particular motor task. This type of analysis is essential if movement experiences are to be planned which will serve to guide and improve each student's individual efforts. The analysis of the result of a movement (product evaluation) provides valuable information relative to the progress a student is making in gaining movement control. The analysis of the characteristics of a movement (process evaluation) provides information about a student's developmental level. Movement is a highly complex area of study, but it is only through observation of each student's characteristics of movement responses, which change from time to time, that progress or lack of progress can be detected. Through carefully planned movement experiences, a student will be able to achieve a level of efficient body movement or movement quality (the refinement of movement). An understanding of this type of evaluation is an important competency for the physical educator.

*Utilization of learning domains.* The fourth component inherent in the basic skills of curriculum design is the understanding and use of the three learning domains. The cognitive taxonomy edited by Bloom (1956), the affective taxonomy authored by Krathwohl, *et al.*, (1964) and the psychomotor taxonomy authored by Harrow (1972) are hierarchical systems for classifying learning outcomes and are suggested for use as frameworks for curriculum development. All educators are responsible for incorporating into the curriculum the skills, abilities, and attitudes relative to affective and cognitive learning. In addition, physical educators, elementary educators and other professionals in the applied and performing arts must incorporate psychomotor abilities into the curriculum. Thus, understanding and use of the taxonomies becomes an important competency in the basic skills of curriculum design.

*Content analysis.* The fifth competency an educator must possess is a thorough understanding of his own discipline, along with the ability to analyze the discipline into sequential units and lessons. With this understanding of the discipline, an educator can help students ascertain the relevance of a particular content area to the practical world and to establish the meaningful relationships that make understanding and retention of content easier.

*Systems analysis.* Once the competency of content area analysis is mastered and levels of learning in the taxonomies are thoroughly understood, an educator can begin the study of systems analysis. In the author's opinion, this is the final competency necessary in the area of curriculum design. It incorporates all the previously discussed skills, enabling the educator to prepare a competency-based curriculum incorporating all desired levels and domains of learning for any given content area.

*Level 1.5: Skills in the*
*Art of Teaching*

The selection of instructional strategies is categorized in this model as 1.5, the "art of teaching." This category incorporates the necessary creativity an effective educator must possess. The variety and relevance of instructional strategies selected to meet the many learning styles of students reflects the educator's depth of comprehension of learning theory and desire to serve as an effective guide for students' mastery learning. Inherent within the "art of teaching" competency are (1) an understanding of affective development as it relates to successful student learning,

(2) an understanding and commitment to the educational philosophy of mastery learning for all students, (3) an understanding and application of motivational theory, (4) integration of learning theory into curriculum design and, (5) interrelating of specific content under study with others to which the student is exposed.

*Understanding affective development.* Educators must be knowledgeable about the affective domain and its implications for successful student achievement. Much emphasis in the "art of teaching" must be placed in the affective area. Helping students restructure attitudes is as important as helping students to acquire information. Attitudes and motivation influence a student's self definition and his impact on others. Therefore, it could logically be stated that before an educator can help a student achieve his ultimate potential in either the cognitive or psychomotor areas, a firm foundation in the affective area must be established. The key to assisting a student in acquiring this foundation is to determine how best to stimulate his interest in learning.

Learning is a continuous process inseparable from living, so long as an individual responds to stimulation. In order for a stimulus to be effective, it must persist sufficiently to arouse a sensory or motor response. This implies that in order for learning to occur, a student's attention must be captured. Attention is a learned response and must be reinforced for expansion of a student's span of attention. For a student to develop an attention span an instructor must identify and control motivators which arouse the student's curiosity. The more success a student experiences the more interest and attention he will acquire for a particular learning situation.

*Application of mastery learning techniques.* Bloom's (1971) theory is composed of five variables for a mastery learning strategy. They are:

1. Determine the student's aptitude for particular kinds of learning.
2. Work toward quality of instruction.
3. Determine the student's ability to understand instruction.

4. Encourage perseverance of the learner.

5. Vary time allowed for learning.

Bloom indicates that student mastery of cognitive learning as well as positive affective consequences increase through instructor awareness and use of mastery learning strategies.

*Application of motivational theory.* Figure 2 reflects a continuum of motivation. A student's interest must first be captured; once you have his attention he can acquire some knowledge. The more satisfaction in terms of success this knowledge/skill level brings to the student, the more appreciation for the activity he or she will develop. From an appreciation, the student begins to structure a set of attitudes toward a particular activity or concept. As the attitude becomes more positive, the student progresses through higher levels of mastery skill development from which can emerge a set of values. It is from a well-developed set of values that changes in life style emerge. It should be evident from Figure 2 that success experiences are one of the important components of

*Figure 2*

*Motivation Continuum: Components
of Affective Development*

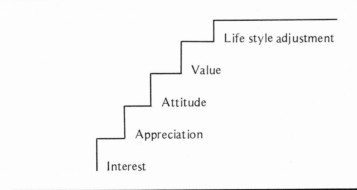

continued learning. To reinforce motivation, it is important to identify the prerequisite experiences necessary for new situations, thereby allowing a student to begin a new learning experience from previous learning. A thorough understanding of this continuum enhances the educator's ability to be effective in the "art of teaching."

*Application of learning theory.* Bugelski (1971) explains the difficulty an educator encounters when trying to apply principles of learning which resulted from laboratory experiments to the real world of the classroom. However, with a thorough understanding of learning theory, educators will be able to select the principles of learning which can be adopted for classroom use and applied to the real world of the learner. According to Bugelski, inherent within any learning theory is an implicit theory of instruction. Bruner's (1966) theory of instruction was designed without specific reference to theories of learning. His model is composed of four major components which tend to be prescriptive. In other words, his model explains *how to improve* learning rather than *how learning actually occurs*. In the opinion of this author, knowledge of how learning occurs and how learning can be improved are essential skills the educator must possess to be effective in the "art of teaching."

*Integration of theory with reality.* As educators we are all accountable for guiding each student toward becoming a well-rounded individual; one who is capable of critical-judgmental thinking, one who is capable of establishing a set of values by which he guides his life and one who is capable of enjoying the ecstasy of the human body through movement experiences. This requires an educator who can integrate into the curriculum specific activities designed to help students interrelate and synthesize experiences into a system of knowledge, values and skills so that learning can become more meaningful and fulfilling. To do this an educator must understand and be able to utilize the three domains of learning in teaching; he must possess the basic skills and creative artistry necessary to become an effective educator.

This model may be summarized succintly in an over-all mission statement followed by the five specific goals:

Mission:  For emerging educators to develop the following specific characteristics identified as essential for effective teaching:

1.1  To develop competencies in communication skills of reading, writing, speaking and moving (body language).

1.2  To develop the ability to utilize and assess learning theories and principles.

1.3  To develop the ability to apply instructional techniques.

1.4  To develop the ability to synthesize a curriculum design package.

1.5  To develop the ability to apply and assess the art of teaching.

## Possibilities for the Future

The basic purposes of education have for many years focused on identifying the qualities that make up civilized man and selecting the competencies he must possess (1) to succeed in society, (2) to develop an appreciation for people and the world around him, and (3) to experience the many joys of living. Inherent within this mission is the development of a thinking, feeling, doing individual.

Futuristic education must focus on greater integration of knowledge. It must be sensitive to the balance between utility and vision, theory and technique, the critical (logical) and the creative, the scientific and the humanistic. It should strive to produce individuals who are capable of maintaining a reflective and rounded view of life along with an area of specialization. With this over-all mission, the harmonious development of the whole individual should emerge as the successful product of education.

Since all educators have this common mission, each must do his share to bring about success. For physical educators, the over-all mission of the new education should be to help each individual develop into an "ultimate athlete" by turning him on to a lifetime of benefits through movement. To achieve this, each individual must be reached with professional assistance in a variety of specialized areas. The new physical education program should provide lifelong physical activities for every individual (body type). It should be designed to help students develop a deep awareness of their own bodies in movement. Ideally, the new physical education will be one where each student develops a good self-image and has success experiences in at least one particular movement activity which will carry over into a life-long leisure pursuit.

The development of a movement activities program (perhaps more usefully called a functional physical education program) must be based upon an awareness of three aspects—first, the analysis of activities from simple to complex; second, the classification of individuals according to abilities from novice to expert; and third, evaluation in terms of present and future use. As movement specialists, physical educators must understand movement as an integral part of life and be able to apply movement to varying life situations as a means of encouraging self-awareness and self-expression. They must understand movement both as a teaching tool and as an art form.

The psychomotor domain taxonomy (Harrow, 1972) serves as a guide by providing a framework for categorizing movement behaviors from simple to complex. Since it is hierarchical in structure, the classification levels establish the boundaries within which movement behavior can be placed. Through unobtrusive observation of student movement behaviors during play activities, informal movement, and testing situations, educators who have a thorough understanding of movement mechanics can identify the existing movement capabilities of the student and correctly place him or her into a given program at the appropriate level.

Formative and summative evaluations of movement behaviors are built into a well designed curriculum through the use of performance objectives. Appropriate assessments, periodically conducted, assist the student in determining success experiences and are necessary for continued growth.

Because people are movement oriented, the primary focus of physical education must center around *learning to move* and *learning through movement*. Two of the major missions of a curriculum focused on movement activities are the following: (1) continuous development of the ability to use the body effectively in increasingly complex tasks with increasing evidence of movement control and quality, and (2) continuous use of movement activities to enhance the individual's discovery of himself, his environment and his world. A curriculum which focuses on learning to move and learning through movement allows the individual to experiment, to practice, to think, to make decisions, to evaluate, to dare and to persist.

Using the psychomotor domain taxonomy as a framework for designing a comprehensive movement program (kindergarten through adult leisure activity), the specific goals of the program are the following:

1. Integration of proprioceptive, motor and perceptual processes.
   a. Enhancement of basic movement patterns
   b. Development of perceptual-motor tasks
   c. Development of body image, capabilities and relationship to space

   Taxonomy Levels:
   1.00 Reflex Movement
   2.00 Basic Fundamental Movement
   3.00 Perceptual Abilities

2. Development of over-all body fitness and health.
   a. Development of muscular strength and endurance
   b. Enhancement of flexibility
   c. Development of cardio-vascular fitness

   Taxonomy Level:
   4.00 Physical Abilities

3. Sophistication of mechanical (movement) tasks and complex movement patterns.

a. Development of efficient body    Taxonomy Level:
   movement                             5.00 Skilled Movement
b. Enhancement of skills move-
   ment

4. Transcendence of self to the ultimate joy of life through movement.
   a. Development of movement    Taxonomy Level:
      imagination                      6.00 Non-discursive Communi-
   b. Development of movement cre-       cation
      ativity
   c. Development of movement life
      values

Although focusing primarily on the education of the physical aspect of the individual, the physical educator deals also with the enhancement of the cognitive and affective development of each individual and the integration of the whole individual. It is important to assist the individual in developing a balance which pays due attention to the demands and needs of the mind as well as the body.

**Summary**

As a result of the impetus provided by the behavioral objectives movement, the entire physical education curriculum from kindergarten through adult leisure activity can be viewed more critically. It can be restructured into developmental stages so that each individual can, in fact, have the opportunity to grow into the "ultimate athlete."

The first stage could be designed around enhancement of basic movement patterns and perceptual abilities. The second stage could be designed around a thorough understanding of physical abilities and their development and maintenance. This would incorporate an understanding of anatomy and physiology, some basic mechanical principles of movement such as center of gravity and force, and an understanding of the effects of exercise on the body. Once the student has developed a satisfactory competency level in stages one and two, he could move into a program of skill development with the assurance of having successful experiences because his mind and body would be prepared for refined skill movement. A three-pronged program such as this could eventually produce the "ultimate athlete." It would better prepare the adult population to maintain a level of physical health and condition conducive to a more productive life style; in addition, leisure pursuits could be more stimulating and challenging.

The physical education program should be a good place in itself for a student to be, not just a passageway through which he moves on to some future life style. A student cannot memorize the future. Rather, he must be able to interact positively with his environment. This means he must be able to care, cope and communicate.

A future dedicated to the idea of cultural and liberating education for students will result in a harmonious balance in the total sense of self. It will encompass the integrated development and functioning of a thinking (cognitive), feeling (affective), doing (psychomotor) individual. It is time to reflect on the past and the present in education and to establish educational goals for the future. It will be these goals for education in the future that will shape our way of life in time to come. We have an obligation to our students to prepare them for the challenges they will face.

## References

Bloom, B.S. (Ed.) *Taxonomy of Educational Objectives: Handbook I, Cognitive Domain*. New York: David McKay Company, Inc., 1956.

Bloom, B.S., J.T. Hastings and G.F. Madaus. *Handbook of Summative and Formative Evaluation of Student Learning*. New York: McGraw-Hill, 1971.

Bruner, J.S. *Toward a Theory of Instruction*. Cambridge, Massachusetts: The Belknap Press of Harvard University Press, 1966.

Bugelski, B.R. *The Psychology of Learning Applied to Teaching*. Indianapolis, Indiana: The Bobbs-Merrill Company, Inc., 1971.

Harrow, A.J. *A Taxonomy of the Psychomotor Domain: A Guide for Developing Behavioral Objectives.* New York: David McKay Company, Inc., 1972.

Krathwohl, D.R. *et al. Taxonomy of Educational Objectives: Handbook II, Affective Domain.* New York: David McKay Company, Inc., 1964.

Leonard, G. *Ultimate Athlete.* New York: Viking Press, Inc., 1975.

McAshan, H.H. *The Goals Approach to Performance Objectives.* Philadelphia, Pennsylvania: W.B. Saunders Company, 1974.

Riles, W.C. Public Expectations. *Proceedings of the Conference on Educational Accountability.* Princeton, New Jersey: Educational Testing Service, March 1971, G1-G5.

Tyler, R.W. Report to American Educational Research Association (mimeographed, n.d.)

# 11.
# A Behavioral Typology
# of Educational Objectives
# for the Cognitive Domain

Reed G. Williams

Those still involved in the behavioral objectives movement are now spending less time in theoretical anticipation of the benefits and weaknesses of behavioral objectives and more effort in reality-testing of the objectives approach. Objectives are being created and used for teaching complex material to real students in actual school systems. This reality-testing phase has resulted in a number of insights and the identification of several issues and problems associated with use of behavioral objectives. This chapter deals with one such problem: developing a mechanism for resolving the discrepancy between the objectives an instructor holds intuitively and those he or she is able to represent in behavioral form.

Gronlund (1970) addressed this problem when he advocated preserving such labels as "understand" and "appreciate" as a basis against which to compare the underlying list of behavioral objectives. This provides a mechanism to help ensure that the behavioral objectives generated adequately represent the intended, more molar, goals of the instructional designer. Our experience at the Southern Illinois University School of Medicine suggests that the problem may be more involved than Gronlund's solution would indicate. Individuals who prepare behavioral objectives are often limited in their objectives-writing experience and in their available time. These limitations often result in a set of objectives which fails to meet the individual's own expectations for students, especially in the area of intellectual process demands.

Another approach to solving this problem is to provide models or blueprints for objectives which tap a variety of intellectual processes. *The Taxonomy of Educational Objectives: Cognitive Domain* (Bloom, 1956) was intended to serve this function and to improve the clarity of communication among people involved in instruction. However, discussions with teachers, instructional designers and educational researchers who have used the taxonomy have revealed some problems which interfere with achieving the original purposes for which it was developed. First, the taxonomy is complex, necessitating a substantial amount of time for initial mastery, and decreasing the likelihood of retention and, therefore, of regular use. Second, even experienced users of the taxonomy have difficulties in agreeing on the classification of objectives or test items into the categories of the taxonomy. Finally, the taxonomic categories generally are defined in terms of the intellectual processes required of learners rather than in terms of the observable characteristics of tasks presented to learners in the form of objectives or test questions. A typology with categories defined in terms of concrete characteristics of tasks structured by teachers not only should lead to better inter-rater agreement in classifying objectives or test items, but also should provide instructors with more guidance in producing tasks or objectives which fit each category.

This chapter presents a typology which defines its categories by casting generic behavioral objectives describing the type(s) of task fitting each classification rather than the intellectual process induced by the task. It is influenced heavily by the original taxonomy (Bloom, 1956), by the conceptual works of Merrill and Boutwell (1973), Gagne (1970), the Maccias (1969) and by the behavioral objectives movement (Mager, 1962; Popham, 1969).

This report describes the typology, discusses its features and the rationale for each, and provides some empirical data regarding inter-rater agreement when using the typology to classify behavioral objectives.

## Description of the Typology

The categories of the typology are based on the assumption that most tasks required of learners have two components: learning task *content* and applying generic intellectual *operations* to that content. To perform the task stated in an objective or required by a test question, the learner must first learn (or have previously learned) certain information basic to and determined by the task. For convenience these basics will be referred to as the *content* of the task. Task content is subdivided into the following types: facts, concepts (classes of objects or events), principles (statements of relationships among objects or events) and procedures (tasks with psychomotor aspects). Because they are commonly used terms, objects and properties of objects have been added as separate entries under content, even though many readers will recognize that these could be subsumed under concepts. The term "events" is listed separately for the same reason.

Operation refers to the way in which the content is used. "A stitch in time saves nine" is an often quoted principle or rule. As such, it is content which is often learned. Once learned, this content may be used in various ways. It may be recited verbatim (Memorization). It may be restated in different words (Summarization). Cases where the rule has been applied may be identified (Instantiation). The rule may be used to anticipate the consequences of certain acts (e.g., sewing or failing to sew up small rips in clothing) (Prediction). The rule or principle may also be used to arrange conditions so that a desired outcome results (Application). Finally, knowledge of the rule may be used in conjunction with values to select the most desirable action in a given situation (Evaluation). These same intellectual operations may be applied to almost all types of content. The exceptions are revealed in Table 1, which introduces the typology.

This system for categorizing objectives is referred to as a typology rather than a taxonomy since no claims are made about the order of the categories. The operations are not ordered in terms of presumed difficulty, nor is there any assumption that successful performance of a task of one type necessarily implies the ability to perform successfully a task which falls into any other category. Put another way, the ability to perform a task which fits one category is neither presumed to be a necessary prerequisite for performance of a task which fits some other category, nor does it necessarily indicate the ability to perform satisfactorily a task in some other category of the typology.

A third dimension, test mode, influences placement of objectives in the typology. Test mode is divided into two classifications using a common distinction in the field of educational measurement. The *recognition* mode refers to selecting from alternative choices as in multiple choice or true-false test items. The *production* mode refers to any task requiring the learner to determine available choices as part of the selection process. All open-ended evaluation procedures, including performance tests which use naturalistic observation as the measurement tool, are included in this mode.

In most cases test mode is independent of operation and content. That is, most combinations of operation and content can be tested in either the recognition or production test mode. In some cases, however, the operation category determines the test mode classification of an objective. The best example is in the application category. Inspection of Table 1 reveals that no application objectives are found in the recognition test mode column. Application, as used in this typology, requires that the learner generate the alternative actions to be considered—a condition which cannot be achieved in the recognition test mode.

Generic behavioral objectives have been used to define each cell in the typology as a convenient means of integrating the three dimensions of the typology and aiding users to identify and/or construct objectives fitting each category. The objectives communicate a general description of the situation to which the learner must respond, the information and tools which should be made available to the learner and the type of behavior required if the learner is to document competency. Users of the typology need only identify or write objectives similar in form with specifics added to correctly classify or construct behavioral objectives or test items.

Inspection of Table 1 reveals that in some cases more than one generic behavioral objective per category exists, thus indicating that these categories may be tested in more than one way. As is always the case, objectives need not take the exact form specified in Table 1 to fit the category. Rather, the generic objectives are written to indicate the combination of elements which must be present if an objective or test item is to fit a particular category.

## Empirical Test of the Typology

As indicated earlier, two major goals for the original taxonomy and for this typology were to improve the clarity of communication among people involved in instruction and to stimulate instruction which encourages the learner's use of a broad range of intellectual abilities. A classification system designed to achieve either of these objectives must be comprised of categories that are clearly enough defined so that two or more individuals can agree on the correct classification of instructional objectives. If this condition is not met, the categories do not have agreed upon (conventional) meanings and clear communication is impossible. Further, it is unlikely under these conditions that the typology communicates clearly enough to systematically increase the breadth of intellectual abilities called for in educational objectives written by users of the typology. Therefore, inter-rater agreement in classifying objectives is one important indicator of the utility of the typology.

A second important test of the typology is to determine whether it provides sufficient categories to cover the range of cognitive abilities used by learners in instructional tasks. Another factor which should be considered in estimating the value of the typology is the amount of training time necessary to prepare an individual to use the typology reliably. An empirical test was devised and conducted to determine how this typology performed according to these three criteria.

*Table 1*

*Behavioral Typology of Educational Objectives*

| Operation | Content | Test Mode: Recognition | Test Mode: Production | Example Objectives |
|---|---|---|---|---|
| Memorization | Facts, Verbal descriptions of: concepts principles procedures events objects properties of objects | Given a cue and a set of alternatives, select the exact replica of information previously learned. | Given a cue, construct an exact replica of information previously learned. | Given the previously studied diagram of body compartments and a list of words identifying each compartment, label each compartment with the appropriate identifying word.<br><br>Name the ganglionic blocking agents commonly used as peripheral vasodilators.<br><br>OTHER EXAMPLES: Recalling normal values, synonyms, definitions of terms, defining attributes of concepts, poetry, drama. |
| Summarization | Facts, Verbal descriptions of: concepts principles procedures events objects properties of objects | 1. Given a paraphrase description, select the correct name for the fact, concept, principle, procedure, event, object or property of an object from a set of alternatives.<br><br>2. Given the name, select the correct paraphrased description of a fact, concept, principle, procedure, event, object or property of an object from a set of alternatives. | 1. Given a paraphrase description, write the correct name for the fact, concept, principle, procedure, event, object or property of an object.<br><br>2. Given the name, write a paraphrased description of the fact, concept, principle, procedure, event, object or property of an object. | Given paraphrase descriptions of optical measurement instruments, select from a list the correct name of each instrument.<br><br>Describe in your own words the four major morphologic patterns of irreversible cell injury or cell death.<br><br>OTHER EXAMPLES: Summarizing events, theories, directives, substance of articles. |
| Instantiation | Concepts principles procedures objects properties of objects | 1. Given the name, select a previously unused example of the concept, principle, procedure, object or property of an object from a set of alternatives. | 1. Given the name, describe a previously unused example of the concept, principle, procedure, object or property of an object. | Give an example, not provided during instruction, of each of the antagonisms listed below: chemical antagonism physiological antagonism |

*(Continued)*

*Table 1 (Continued)*

| Operation | Content | Test Mode: Recognition | Test Mode: Production | Example Objectives |
|---|---|---|---|---|
| Instantiation (cont'd) | | | | pharmacological antagonism<br>non-competitive (non-specific) antagonism |
| | | 2. Given a previously unused example of the concept, principle, procedure, object or property of an object, select the correct name from a set of alternatives. | 2. Given a previously unused example of the concept, principle, procedure, object or property of an object, name it. | Given any electron microscope slide of an injured or dead cell, locate the following major ultra-structural changes:<br>(1) swelling of mitochondria<br>(2) course granules in mitochondria<br>(3) thickening of plasma membrane<br>(4) formation of bleks<br>(5) creation of myeline figures<br>(6) distortion of microvilli<br>(7) deterioration of desmosomes.<br><br>OTHER EXAMPLES: Identifying patterns of events. Identifying patterns in data. |
| Prediction | Concepts | Given some of the defining characteristics of an object, select other expected characteristics from a list. | Given some of the defining characteristics of an object, list other expected characteristics. | Given a case history and physical exam findings, predict what findings you would expect on a radiograph. |
| | Principles | Given a previously unused description of a situation/event with the antecedent conditions of a relationship embedded, select from alternatives the most likely consequences. | Given a previously unused description of a situation/event with the antecedent conditions of a relationship embedded, describe the most likely consequences. | Given biographical information about residents of a precinct, descriptions of successful and unsuccessful candidates in the precinct in prior elections, and descriptions of candidates currently running for office, name the candidate most likely to win the election. |
| | | Given a previously unused description of outcomes (consequences), select from alternatives the ordered set of ante- | | Given a medical sign or symptom and a list of all sites where a lesion might exist, name the sites of lesions which would pro- |

*(Continued)*

*Table 1 (Continued)*

| Operation | Content | Test Mode: Recognition | Test Mode: Production | Example Objectives |
|---|---|---|---|---|
| **Prediction** (cont'd) | Principles (cont'd) | cedent conditions which would achieve that outcome. | | duce that sign or symptom and give a sound physiological explanation as to how a lesion in each site could cause the resultant symptom. |
| | Procedures | Given a previously unused description of a situation in which a procedure is applied, select from alternatives the most likely outcome. | Given a previously unused description of a situation in which a procedure is applied, describe the most likely outcome. | Given the description of a hypotensive patient, predict the actions of therapeutic doses of norepinephrine on cardiac output. |
| | | Given a previously unused description of outcomes (consequences), select from alternatives the ordered set of procedures which would achieve that outcome. | | OTHER EXAMPLES: Predicting correct spelling of previously unseen words through knowledge of rules. Predicting amount of time necessary to accomplish anything given knowledge of conditions. |
| **Application** | Concepts Principles | | Given a previously unused case/problem and a desired outcome, arrange the antecedent conditions necessary to achieve that outcome. (Less preferred alternative: describe the antecedent conditions necessary to achieve that outcome.) | Given results from a history, physical and a laboratory workup for a patient with any of the listed diseases or disorders (diagnosis unknown to the student): Order or describe appropriate preventative measures and/or therapeutic regimens for preventing or altering the disease. |
| | Procedures | | Given a previously unused case/problem and a desired outcome, perform the procedures necessary to achieve that outcome. (Less preferred alternative: describe the steps in using procedures necessary to achieve that outcome.) | Given any patient symptom, describe the procedure necessary to determine if the symptom is an adverse reaction due to drug–drug interaction rather than a disease manifestation. OTHER EXAMPLES: Arranging effective marketing procedures. Building a better mousetrap. |

*(Continued)*

*Table 1 (Continued)*

| Operation | Content | Test Mode: Recognition | Test Mode: Production | Example Objectives |
|---|---|---|---|---|
| Evaluation | Principles Procedures | Given a description of a situation, a list of alternative actions and the criteria/values upon which to base the action, select the most desirable action. | | You want to measure the level of a constituent $(x)$ of cerebrospinal fluid and have decided that a spectrophotometer is the instrument of choice in this particular case. You must carefully select a technique to make a quantitative measurement. |
| | | | Given a description of a situation and a list of alternative actions, name the most desirable action and describe the criteria/values on which your decision was based. | (a) List possible experimental techniques that you could attempt to resolve the problem. <br> (b) Describe the most appropriate technique, and describe the criteria on which your decision was based. |
| | | | Given a description of a situation, list the alternative actions available, name the most desirable action and describe the criteria/values on which your decision was based. | OTHER EXAMPLES: Judging quality of products. Judging communications in terms of accuracy, internal consistency, etc. |

Nine objectives were selected from existing sources by the author and modified when necessary to fit the definitions in the typology. The objectives were then classified by the author using the six operation categories. Objectives were selected to provide at least one representative of each operation category. Two representatives were selected in each of three categories.

In addition, the author asked a colleague who had not seen the typology to select nine objectives from existing sources which "represented the spectrum of intellectual operations required of learners." The only qualifications were that the objectives be limited to the cognitive domain and meet the criteria for well-formed behavioral objectives (Mager, 1962). The author then classified these objectives using the typology discussed above. (The 18 objectives used for the empirical test are available from the author. Some of the objectives now appear as examples in Table 1. These objectives were substituted for examples used in the original typology after the empirical test was completed.)

Thirteen individuals with experience in writing and helping people write behavioral objectives were asked to study the typology and classify each objective. Some of these individuals had prior experience working with Bloom's Taxonomy, but most did not. None of them had prior experience with the typology.

Table 2 represents the results of this empirical test. The individuals involved reported that it took from 20 minutes to one hour to study the typology and classify the 18 objectives.

Looking at the nine objectives selected by the author to fit the categories of the typology, decisions by seven of the 13 raters agreed completely with those of the author. Only 15 misclassifications were made in 117 decisions. Nine of these misclassifications were made by two individuals.

Individuals involved in the empirical test had been instructed to designate a second choice when they were unsure of the proper classification. In the case of the 15 errors, three were accompanied by a second choice that was correct.

Thus, it appears that with little training time, independent

## *Table 2*

## *Results of the Empirical Test of the Typology*

| | Objective | Author's Categorization | No. of Raters Selecting Each Category | | | | | | Predominant Categorization |
|---|---|---|---|---|---|---|---|---|---|
| | | | M | S | I | P | A | E | |
| Objectives Selected to Fit the Categories of the Typology | 1 | S | 3 | 10 | — | — | — | — | S |
| | 2 | M | 12 | 1 | — | — | — | — | M |
| | 3 | P | — | — | — | 13 | — | — | P |
| | 4 | E | — | — | 2 | — | — | 11 | E |
| | 5 | I | 2 | — | 11 | — | — | — | I |
| | 6 | M | 13 | — | — | — | — | — | M |
| | 7 | A | — | — | — | — | 12 | 1 | A |
| | 8 | P | 1 | — | — | 11 | — | 1 | P |
| | 9 | E | — | — | — | 1 | 3 | 9 | E |
| Objectives Selected to Cover the Cognitive Domain Without Knowledge of the Typology | 10 | I | 7 | — | 5 | — | — | 1 | M |
| | 11 | I | 10 | — | 3 | — | — | — | M |
| | 12 | P | — | 2 | 1 | 8 | 2 | — | P |
| | 13 | A | 1 | — | 2 | 1 | 7 | 2 | A |
| | 14 | I | 3 | 3 | 5 | — | 1 | 1 | I |
| | 15 | P | — | — | — | 11 | 1 | 1 | P |
| | 16 | M | 9 | 4 | — | — | — | — | M |
| | 17 | I | 2 | 2 | 4 | 1 | 3 | 1 | I |
| | 18 | A | — | — | 1 | — | 12 | — | A |

| | | | | | | | |
|---|---|---|---|---|---|---|---|
| M | = | Memorization | S | = Summarization | I | = | Instantiation |
| P | = | Prediction | A | = Application | E | = | Evaluation |

raters can classify objectives selected or written to fit categories with a high level of agreement. The typology performs well in this regard.

How about inter-rater agreement in classifying objectives not written to fit the typology categories? This is a much stiffer test of the typology, since it does not allow the increase in clarity of communication which can be derived by writing objectives according to the standards established in the various classification definitions. With this set of objectives, none of the raters agreed with the author on every decision. For the 13 raters, 53 of 117 decisions deviated from those of the author. In fact, the author was among the minority in his classification of two objectives, resulting in 17 decisions being recorded as errors.

In all, 33 of the 53 "incorrect" decisions appear to be attributable to unclearly stated objectives or to objectives containing too little information for adequate classification. Bloom (1956, p. 21) has identified these as major problems in using the original taxonomy also. However, problems such as these are easily identified and solved with the present typology. Twenty one errors of classification could have been avoided with the addition of a total of five words to three objectives. The others could have been avoided with slightly more involved rewriting. Use of the typology in constructing the objectives would have reduced or eliminated these problems.

A more important consideration regarding the objectives selected to cover the domain of cognitive abilities concerns the rater's ability to classify each objective using the typology. Every objective was fitted into some category of the typology by every rater. None of the raters commented that an objective failed to match a category. Thus, it appears that the typology fits cognitive abilities described in the domain of behavioral objectives available to the author.

## Summary
Preliminary studies of the typology of cognitive educational

objectives represented here suggest that the typology may be a useful tool for instructors, instructional designers and researchers. The typology can be used efficiently.

Raters were easily able to fit objectives selected as representing the range of intellectual abilities into categories of the typology.

Use of the typology to classify objectives which have been selected to fit the general specifications for each category has demonstrated that such objectives can be classified with a high level of inter-rater agreement. The degree of inter-rater agreement is all the more impressive given the fact that the objectives were written by individuals not familiar with the typology. Objectives were selected because they contained the components specified in the category definition, but they were not rewritten to use certain behavioral verbs or to match examples.

Efforts by raters to agree on the classification of those objectives selected to represent the range of intellectual abilities, but not screened to meet the general specifications for each category, were less successful. However, 62 percent of the errors were the result of unclear or incomplete objectives. Perhaps the most important feature of this typology is that the category definitions themselves suggest changes which will clarify objectives and improve inter-rater agreement in classification of the revised objectives.

The empirical test of the typology did reveal the need to clarify the distinction between the operations categories, application and evaluation. This distinction has been sharpened in the version of the typology printed here.

Anecdotal evidence collected from individuals who have seen and/or used the typology suggests that it will have value in aiding instructors and instructional designers to increase the range of cognitive abilities called forth by behavioral objectives. The typology not only helps individuals see new possibilities, but also directs the process of writing objectives which will elicit this competency on the part of students.

## References

Bloom, B.S. (Ed.) *Taxonomy of Educational Objectives: Handbook I: Cognitive Domain.* New York: David McKay, 1956.

Gagne, R.M. *The Conditions of Learning.* New York: Holt, Rinehart and Winston, 1970.

Gronlund, N.E. *Stating Behavioral Objectives for Classroom Instruction.* Toronto, Canada: Collier-MacMillan, 1970.

Maccia, E.S. and G.S. Maccia. Personal Communication. Department of History and Philosophy of Education, Indiana University at Bloomington, 1969.

Mager, R.F. *Preparing Instructional Objectives.* Palo Alto: Fearon Publishers, 1962.

Merrill, M.D. and Boutwell, R.C. Instructional Development: Methodology and Research. In Kerlinger, F.N. (Ed.), *Review of Research in Education Vol. 1.* Itasca, Ill.: F.E. Peacock, 1973.

Popham, W.J. Objectives and Instruction. *AERA Monograph Series on Curriculum Evaluation,* 1969, No. 3, 32-52.

Development of this typology was supported in part by a grant from the Fund for Improvement of Postsecondary Education, Department of Health, Education and Welfare. The author acknowledges the assistance of Kay Bleach, Lynn Kienzler, Janet McDole, M. David Merrill, Linda Oberline, Gerry Schermerhorn, John Shatzer and David L. Silber in preparing the typology and/or manuscript.